First-Time Entrepreneur?

*Set your strategy, master your mindset and
turn your business idea into reality!*

Kirsty Knight

ISBN: 978-1-8382280-1-9 Paperback

FREE ACTIONABLE STEPS WORKBOOK

Just to say thanks for buying my book, I would like to give you the

Actionable Steps Workbook PDF

that goes along with this book, so you can take your time to work through them, 100% FREE!.

TO DOWNLOAD GO TO:

https://kirstyknightcoaching.com/first-time-entrepreneur/

DEDICATION

I would like to dedicate this book to the following people:

My parents, Jan and Keith

For instilling the belief into my sister and I, that we were capable of achieving anything we wanted in life; for being such fun to be around; and for their continued support, help and guidance with everything I attempt to accomplish. I'm grateful for everything they've taught me and continue to teach me.

The love of my life, Andrew

For being my biggest supporter. He puts up with my incessant chatter, my overexcitability for random new business ideas and my unquenchable thirst for travel and sunshine. I am eternally grateful for all the things he does and all the things he is and couldn't imagine sharing my life with anyone else.

My big sister, Jess

For being the best sister I could have had growing up, a 'techy' and organized business partner and for always making me laugh.

My partner's family, Tim, Karl, Jayne and Becki

For their continued support and help, with both their tools and talents, with our small business, particularly when our requests are made last minute!

"Build your own dreams, or someone else will hire you to build theirs."

—Farrah Gray

Contents

INTRODUCTION 11

CHAPTER 1: STARTING YOUR BUSINESS 15
CHAPTER 2: MARKETING YOUR BUSINESS 41
CHAPTER 3: THE EARLY DAYS OF YOUR BUSINESS 69
CHAPTER 4: INVESTING IN YOURSELF 81
CHAPTER 5: CREATING A BUSINESS NOT A JOB 92
CHAPTER 6: YOUR MINDSET IS EVERYTHING 112

CONCLUSION 135
NEXT STEPS 137
ACKNOWLEDGEMENTS 141
ABOUT THE AUTHOR 143

INTRODUCTION

I always knew I wanted to be an entrepreneur. It was on my 'when I grow up…' list from an early age. Admittedly, this was nestled between several other random ideas that I wanted to have a go at (novelist, spy, ice-skating cook – don't ask), which would now probably be acceptable (since the terms 'multipassionate' and 'multipotentialite' have been coined), but at the time made me seem like I was an overly ambitious, totally confused little girl with no apparent direction in life.

I dropped several of these random ideas from my list, but the one that always seemed to remain was the desire to set up and run my own business. This desire most likely originated from my dad. He warned us repeatedly against becoming dependent on others for our earnings and encouraged us to create a life where we are rewarded by our own efforts, rather than putting money in someone else's pocket. He was a self-made, hard-working farmer at the time and over the years had added many trades to his belt – always so he could be totally self-sufficient, self-employed, and as far away as you could possibly be from dependent on someone else for his money. He practiced what he preached. And his messaging clearly found its way into my subconscious.

At 25 years old, however, despite having worked as a freelance/self-employed construction project manager for several years, taking on a massive barn conversion project when I had zero experience or knowledge in that field, and accepting the deal that I would only make money if the project netted a decent value at the end (which some might consider to be the typical risk taking, go-getter attitude of an entrepreneur in the making), I still wasn't quite living up to my own definition of 'an entrepreneur'. I felt there was a difference between being a freelancer/self-employed and creating a business that ultimately could provide a product or service without you being present. Of course, since a lot of freelancers do eventually expand their businesses beyond themselves, still have to manage their finances and market themselves, and do all the same core business tasks, I now realize that this was more down to my own mindset blocks than it was the actual facts. It is entirely up to you whether or not you want to call yourself a small business owner, an entrepreneur, or a freelancer.

Another mindset issue I was having that contributed to me not seeing myself as a 'proper' entrepreneur was the psychological phenomenon— imposter syndrome. I was completely unable to believe that I had achieved the freelance job legitimately, because of my own efforts and skills. The work was for family-friends and I felt that I had only landed the job because of those connections, along with the fact I was the person proposing the idea. This meant there had been no requirement for me to do any marketing, branding or sales pitches to get the job. Also, as they trusted me to deliver the project successfully, there were also no accountability checks, quality checks, or even formal project meetings and updates I had to endure. They essentially gave me free rein. This obviously removed a huge amount of red tape, which meant I really could just focus on the job at hand. I took the opportunity to get way more involved in the day-to-day running of the projects (I properly got my hands dirty—plumbing, digging, compacting, pointing, decorating, floor laying—you name it, I had a go) and as a result created a much bigger profit margin at the end. So, happiness was had all around. But it did nothing for my confidence that I could run a business myself, set up formal systems, do marketing, or work with the public in a 'proper' formal setting.

In hindsight, I can view the outcome differently. I could have taken the experience to demonstrate that you don't need fancy formal systems, corporate red tape, and bureaucracy to deliver a successful outcome. I could have acknowledged that many skills used in project management are similar to those used in business. But at the time, as with many things in life, I just couldn't see it.

I felt like I still had not ticked off that 'bucket list' item of having and running my own 'proper' business.

It wasn't that I was short of ideas. I had loads of great ideas. I could easily spot trends in the market and by assessing our skills, experience, and what assets we had available to us, I could easily see how to convert many of them into opportunities. But I didn't know which one was the 'right one'. I also felt like I didn't have one specific key strength/skill to guide my search. I didn't consider myself to be an expert in any area. I hadn't had 15 years as a strategic analyst or 25 years in PR, like a lot of other older entrepreneurs had, so there was no obvious path for me to go down.

All of this did nothing for me, other than to make me feel totally and utterly stuck. I was still working and undertaking other random projects here and there, which I enjoyed. But deep down I felt very disappointed in myself because I hadn't taken the plunge and started my own 'proper' business yet.

Fast-forward six years and I am the owner of a small, yet profitable camping and glamping (camping but more glamorous—you don't need to bring your own tent) business, a partner in a small holiday lettings and furnishing business, and I have a life and business coaching practice helping other first-time entrepreneurs create a business and life they love.

I'm not telling you this to boast. Far from it. I feel I am still very much at the bottom of a very steep mountain with huge projects and opportunities ahead of me that I'm not quite able to reach yet, and I am still shaping my businesses into what I want them to be. Rather, I tell you this because I finally did get the opportunity and push that I needed to start my first business. If I hadn't, I would still be searching for my mountain.

I want to help you find your mountain. But faster and with fewer mistakes. I don't want you to waste any more time before you take that leap into your first business, if you haven't already.

And so, I have condensed the valuable lessons I learned in my business journey. It isn't a comprehensive step-by-step guide of how to start your business, but it should be food for thought and highlight a clear pathway for what you need to figure out on your journey. I am hoping that it will give you the inspiration and motivation to take that leap and start your first business, as well as some practical tools to figure out the business basics along the way. I'm only a few steps ahead of you, so I am confident that if I can do it, you can too.

CHAPTER I
STARTING YOUR BUSINESS

So how did I finally start my first business? First, I actually made the decision that I wanted (more than anything) to start my own business and that I should do it now. A simple enough decision, but toying with the idea of it and feeling disappointed in myself that I hadn't done it yet clearly wasn't making me commit to it. I had to officially make that decision. So, I did. I had waited long enough.

I then brainstormed ideas that my partner and I could work together on. We looked at things that were becoming fashionable and trendy, like the tiny house movement and the trend toward having a garden office. My partner is an architect and is handy with a hammer, so we figured we could use his skills to design some cool cabin-like structures to sell. Another of the trends was the glamping trend. Typically this was some sort of quirky accommodation set up in a beautiful spot in nature that was rented out for guests to stay in—sometimes a tent, other times a shepherd's hut—that had full amenities (like furniture sets, bedding, crockery, cooking equipment, and gas stoves). I had helped my mother out years earlier with cleaning and prepping her holiday rentals and had also worked as a waitress and bar supervisor for several years, so I figured customer service and hospitality were within my skillset. We then started to get excited—combining both of our skillsets and the opportunities available to us led us to the idea that my partner could design and build some quirky cabins, we could put them on my parent's farm, and let them out for guests to stay in.

A brief mention of this idea to my mother, and she told me of someone she knew who owned some cabins they rented out to guests. We figured this was the perfect opportunity to do some research and decide if we could indeed do this type of business. A few clicks later and we had booked our weekend stay in a cabin, not too far from our hometown. The weekend proved very useful—we could see the infrastructure required to provide a decent quality service to the guests; we could assess our own experiences as guests, what we liked and didn't like, what we could do differently; and we could chat with the other guests and see that they appreciated the space and type of holiday they had bought. Back at home, we brainstormed more ideas for our new business, with the plan being that we would start the following year but would take this year to iron out all the details in a business plan.

And then life happened. We got busy with the projects we were working on already. We pushed our idea to the side while we dealt with our day-to-day. Two weeks later, we had made zero progress toward completing our business plan. I'm guessing it would have stayed that way for quite a while, if it hadn't been for what happened next.

A couple of weeks after our cabin stay, around midmorning, the phone rang. It was my dad. He was on his way back from a farm site visit—he was also a renewable energy consultant who helped other farmers put up wind turbines on their land. He had something exciting to tell us. "Put the coffee on," he said, "and I will be there in five." My dad is not one for small talk and chit chat, so I could tell this was something big. Five minutes later, he was in my kitchen with flushed cheeks and a glint in his eye. He excitedly told us that on his way back from his site visit, he had passed a small farm campsite offering 'glamping' stays, and he felt curious to see exactly what we were getting ourselves into. So, he had gone in to have a chat with the owner about it. As it turns out, no one was on site besides a friendly family of campers, who spotted my dad looking a bit lost and had gone over to him to say hi. They were guests of this campsite, staying in one of the glamping units (which turned out to be a canvas bell tent). When dad told them what we were thinking of doing, they excitedly showed us how cool it actually was to stay somewhere off the beaten track like this, how much they loved their tent, what was provided for them, and the facilities they could use.

It was clear that this family was stoked to have found such a place. They were happy enough with just having someone else set up a tent for them, so they didn't have to bring anything themselves.

Then, in no uncertain terms, dad told us he thought we should just start with tents, similar to this other campsite, see if we liked what we are doing and if people liked what we were offering, and then do cabins later. Why waste money and time building a cabin when we didn't even know if people would want to stay in our location? He had a good point.

He asked, "What are you waiting for?"

I told him, "Dad, we have already missed most of the summer and the start of the school holidays, so I'm not sure we could set anything up in time."

He said, "Just get an advert out there and see what kind of interest you get".

What a ridiculous suggestion, I thought, incredulously. We haven't got anything to advertise. It's just a field. "And what if we get a booking for next week?" I asked.

He said confidently, "If you get a booking, I'll help you build the shower and toilet myself."

And with that, he left.

After a moment of stunned silence, a sneaky thought crept in, *maybe he was right.* He had made good points. What if we spent all that time and money building cabins, and then people didn't want cabins? Or they didn't like our farm? Or our location? I figured we should probably test the market first.

And so, I did. I found a photo of a bell tent on Google to use. (Shhh!) I nipped up to the field and took a photo there. My partner made a few changes on Photoshop. I found a glamping site directory and paid for a single advert. I wrote a paragraph that started something like, "Gorgeous bell tent accommodation in a sunny wildflower meadow, set on our small farm in the countryside…hot showers, composting toilet…etc." I hit 'Submit', then ordered a single tent from a bell tent company I found on Google.

After that, I forgot all about it. My partner and I headed off for the weekend with friends. It was only on the way back that I checked my emails. I couldn't believe my eyes. I had an email inquiry for a stay on Tuesday—two days away. My head was spinning. My heart was pounding. I wondered, *could we possibly do this?* I pulled out a notebook and wrote down a list of all the things we would have to do, buy, and build to give our guests a successful glamping experience. The list filled two pages! And they weren't small things. The tasks were things like:

- Move sheep out of field

- Lay water pipe to field

- Build a composting toilet

- Build a shower

- Build a washing up area

- Set up tent

- Make a firepit

- Buy all bedding

- Buy mattresses

- Buy linen

- Sort out lighting

- Make signs

- Source hamper

And on, and on. There was absolutely no way we could do all those things in two days. Feeling disappointed and filled with regret, I emailed the family back, "I'm so sorry but we are booked for those dates. Are there any other dates you could do?" Their reply was no.

I was immediately disheartened. We had missed out on our first customer. Who knew if or when we were going to get a second one? An irrational thought, I know. Less than 40 minutes later, we had our second inquiry. This time they wanted to stay from the Thursday. I thought, *that's a whole two days later!* I quickly rang my dad this time, to tell him and ask him if he would be good to his word and help us—and whether he reckoned we could actually get it ready by Thursday. He said, "Hell yeah!"

And so, with a reckless glint in my eye and an unbounded excitement, I accepted their booking.

The following four days were absolutely ridiculous! They were filled with manic (or panic, I guess) buying, ordering, researching, shopping, building, digging, clearing, welding, plumbing, sawing…you name it, we did it. My mother, father, aunt, partner, and I worked non-stop for four days straight. Even my partner's father, mother, and sister all got roped in to help. It was a mammoth team effort to get the bell tent set up, furnished and looking lovely, the toilet and shower in place and working, and an outside space the guests could enjoy and have their campfire in.

Bang on the dot at 4pm, as I was tightening the last nut on the sink waste pipe, and my partner was fixing the last roofing sheet on the shower, our first guests were trundling down the field toward us. We had started our very own business!

* * *

Positives vs. Negatives of Being an Entrepreneur

Before I tell you why you should start your business right now, I need to make sure that you know exactly what it is that you are getting into. Now I hear you, you picked up this book, you know what it means, yada yada. I thought I did too. I knew that it would entail some hard work, some sacrifices, and that there was the possibility we might fail or not make that much money for a while. Despite that, I still believed deep down that if I could offer a great product or service, after the first year or so I would be raking it in (or at least be making money easily) and could soon join the club of those cocktail-sipping, laptop-wielding, sun-bronzed, highly attractive entrepreneurs who seem to be able to only work a few hours a day on a laptop, on a beach in Bali for 90% of the year. Maybe I was the only one thinking this, but one thing that became blatantly clear as we went through the entrepreneurial journey of our first business was that you really should understand what it is that you are getting into, before you get into it. **Because it isn't for everyone. And it isn't all easy.**

The positives of having your own business are so many. To name just a few:

- You are your own boss

- You have the freedom to choose what to do at any given moment in time

- The money you make goes directly to you and your business

- You don't have anyone else telling you what to do

- You can't be fired

- You don't have to ask permission to go on holiday

- You can decide when to open and close your doors

- You don't have to play by anyone else's rules

- You can delegate certain tasks to take them off your plate

- You get to keep all the praise and satisfaction, as you created it all

- You can work in almost any industry

- It is the fastest way to wealth

- You can contribute to the world, not just by providing a quality product or service, but also by using the proceeds of your business to support a great cause (if you so desire)

But then there are the negatives. These include:

- You have to figure out a way to motivate yourself as your own boss (this is harder than you think)

- If you don't have staff generating value for you, you don't make money when you aren't working

- Your paycheck may not reflect the amount of work you put in at first

- You will still have friends and family telling you what you should be doing

- You will criticize yourself and you will have customers or clients who will do the same

- You don't have the security of a recurring monthly income

- You don't get paid holiday/sick/maternity leave

- You can lose your business

- You have to fight the urge to go on holiday all the time

- You have to fight for a work-life balance (this is also harder than you think)

- You will have legislation and customer service protections that will dictate your rules and taxes and potential business rates to pay

- You have to pay someone to delegate the tasks you want off your plate

- You take full responsibility if your business fails or your product/service isn't good enough

It is important to think about the positives and negatives of starting your own business before you take that leap, so you can make an informed decision about whether it truly is what you want.

I must admit that although I had the general sense that running a business would have its own challenges, when I picked the idea to start a camping and glamping business I thought it would be an easy way to make money. People literally pay you hotel prices to stay in a tent—in a field, no less! It looked like a no brainer. We quickly realized that it was much harder than it looked.

Having said that, I still would rather be a business owner than an employee. But I advise that you sit down and figure out if it really is the right path for you. When business is booming and your business is doing really well a few years down the line, you can start to reap the rewards and enjoy more of the benefits. But in the early days, you need to be willing to have both sides of the coin. Don't be fooled by thinking the grass is simply greener! **The grass is greener where you water it.**

Figure Out Your 'Why'.

Once you have seriously considered both the good parts and the not so good parts of being an entrepreneur, you should then figure out a good reason as to why you have gone down the entrepreneurial path. This has to be more than just deciding that the benefits outweigh the costs for you. This has to be the deeper purpose for why you want to become an entrepreneur.

One exercise you can do to dig out your deeper reason behind starting your own business, coined by Dean Graziosi, is called the Seven Levels Deep exercise. Start by asking yourself why you want to start your own business. Once you have your answer, interrogate that answer with another 'why'. Continue interrogating each answer and move progressively deeper by asking 'why' seven times. This process allows us to move deeper because often we have surface level reasons for doing what we do, but underneath there is always a deeper subconscious thought behind it. After seven 'why's' you will have found a core reason behind everything, one which is usually grounded strongly in an emotion for you. Tapping into that emotion and knowing that deepest 'why' behind what you are doing will motivate you through even the toughest times in your new venture.

Why Haven't You Started Yet?

If you have set your mind on becoming a business owner, but haven't started your first business yet, you can typically be sorted into one of the following categories of first-time entrepreneurs:

1. You have tons of ideas and you can't decide on one

2. You have no idea of what you could do as a business

3. You have an idea, but you don't think it's the 'right' one

4. You aren't ready to start your business because you lack the skills to begin

5. You know what you want to do, but don't know where to start

6. You have it all figured out, but are making excuses instead of getting started

You need to notice that each category is just an excuse. These excuses do nothing to serve you and do not take you toward the dream life and business you want.

Other typical excuses that come up regularly when I ask people why they aren't business owners yet:

- I don't have any contacts

- I don't have the money to start

- I don't have the time

- Now isn't a good time

- I haven't planned it all out yet

- I don't know what my 'one passion' is

- There are already loads of similar businesses out there/it's been done already

- I'm not sure this is the right business to go into for me

I am not judging. Well, I am. But I can empathize with you. I made several of these excuses too. I thought I needed to find the 'right' idea before I got started. And as I had so many interests, I didn't know which one that was. I think I thought the 'right one' would suddenly come to me, and I would have an epiphany that proclaimed, *this is it*. I now believe that there is no such thing as a 'right' idea at the start. It's all about the execution and whether or not you can make it work. In the words of Robert Jordan, "Execution is everything. Even if you start a business with the wrong idea or too many competitors, you can out-execute all the better ideas in the right market." The beauty of being an entrepreneur is that you get to just decide that an idea is the 'right' one to try and go for it. If it doesn't work, then you learn from your mistakes and try again with a different version.

In the end, I decided that I was just going to go for it with that one idea. And I am so glad I did. **Because I would still be waiting for that 'right' idea now if I hadn't.**

Why You Should Start Now

I strongly believe that now is such a great time to be in business. Probably more than ever before. Whatever your business is in, you will find many of these will apply and help you way more than if you had set up 100 years ago. It's easier and cheaper than ever to:

- Gain knowledge on *anything* (Google it)

- Get funding (GoFundMe/Kickstarter/loans/grants)

- Connect and network with others (Facebook, LinkedIn, Instagram, etc.)

- Figure out trends and good ideas (Google/social media analytics)

- Market your product/service (traditional or internet marketing)

- Get information on competition (online)

- Find your ideal customer (online connections are golden)

- Deal with administrative tasks and customer service (online, automated systems, apps, technology, virtually)

- Deliver services and products (online, speedy couriers)

- Get training/qualifications (online and in person)

Also, there are heaps of autobiographies and business books written by successful business owners, which explain the step-by-step instructions to start and grow your business in all areas of industry, and there are business coaches galore available to help you. (Shameless plug—you're reading one of those books by one of those coaches right now!)

So really, what is left? Just your excuses!

Tips for Getting Started

Starting our business the way we did was both exhilarating and extraordinary; it set us on the path to become who we are today. I am super proud of how we took the leap (or rather learned quickly how to fly once we were pushed—by the way, thanks dad), but with hindsight I can now recommend (from first-hand experience) that you start your business slightly differently.

I will outline what we did right and what I strongly recommend you do with yours.

- We considered our experience and skills.

- We considered the lifestyle aspect of it and chose a business that suited the way that we wanted to live.

- We looked at what assets we had available to us already.

- We assessed the timing of when the service would be popular.

- We ensured we had a small sum of money set aside, so we didn't need to borrow money/go into debt just to trial it.

- We knew that our service was trendy and that there was competition, which meant there was definitely a market for it (we were not testing a brand new idea).

- We had researched the competition and experienced the service ourselves (so we knew the bare minimum of what we had to offer, the price, how to deliver it and what was involved).

- We started small, so that if we did fail, we wouldn't lose any more than we were comfortable with.

These are all what I would consider essential first steps when looking to start your business. Beyond this, I strongly advocate for the following:

Don't Wait

If you are now super excited about taking that leap and starting your first business, don't wait to get started. Don't wait for the perfect time. While for some products and services, there may be a better time to launch than others (e.g. opening our bell tents in December would have been pointless), when it comes to your personal life, there is no perfect time to start your first business. We both had other big projects to juggle on top of the extra tasks that came along because of starting the campsite. But we also would have had just as many projects taking up our time the following year, and the year after that, and the year after that. **The time is now.** You only live once and waiting for the perfect time is letting your life pass you by. You have to make time for the things you want to do in life or accept the fact that you will never have them. In the words of Napoleon Hill, "Do not wait: the time will never be 'just right'".

I also truly believe that if we had given ourselves a leisurely whole year to come up with a fully comprehensive business plan for our business, despite our excitement, we would have lost our enthusiasm, let doubt creep in, let life overtake us, and it never would have gotten done. This happened with lots of my ideas prior to the glamping one. I would have a good idea, get all excited, do some research, and then self-doubt would creep in, life and bigger priorities would get in the way, and I would lose momentum, motivation, and give up on the whole idea.

Even if we had managed to draw up that fancy business plan and line everything up in a year, we would have lost a year's worth of learning and growing. In fact, we could have missed the opportunity altogether. Our business plan might also have become completely redundant a year later, if the trend was moving that quickly, so we would have had to start all over again, researching the competitors, reassessing rising costs…etc. I found that the 'perfect' time to start was when we made the decision that it was time, rolled up our sleeves, and made it work.

Make an Informed Business Plan (Without Going Overboard and Stalling Progress)

Now, I am not saying start a business without a plan. **Failing to plan is planning to fail.** But there is a difference between doing a formal, comprehensive, and tedious business plan that takes upwards of a year to complete and doing a responsive, current, snappy business plan that is relevant to where your business is now and has room to grow with you. This should be informed by testing your market first. You can test your market by creating the smallest possible, while still viable, product or service to offer to your target clientele and seeing how it sells, taking notes to make changes and inform future products/services. You see this all the time with Kickstarter campaigns, test product journals, and beta readers (for books and courses). The experience of testing your market will also help you confirm that you actually enjoy what you are creating and doing. This will also show you if owning a business is for you, without having sold your soul to get there.

There is just no point spending hours typing up a business plan for a home-based bakery simply because it seems trendy. You might not actually enjoy baking bread and you have not tested your baking on real people yet—your family doesn't count (they are biased and may not feel comfortable being honest). You would be better off deciding how much time and money you are willing to put into testing this idea, then finding a customer, baking the bread for them, and having them give you feedback on taste, your location, the idea, the price…etc.

Only after you have done multiple rounds of this testing can you sit down and analyze the market, the competition, how you need to tweak your product or service, how to find and serve your market, your facilities, the operations, the what if's, your strategy, the costs, your budget, your personal living budget, your breakeven point…etc., which you will then put into a plan that you can show to a potential investor if needed. They are likely to be much more willing to invest if you have demonstrated that you have tested the market, that there is a need, and you have shown your commitment to making your business work.

A quick note here on testing your product/service and conducting market research—people tend to overcomplicate this part of it. You really don't need to overthink it. A quick Google search will bring up other competitors that you can click through. You can then purchase from your competitors to see what kind of experience they are giving. You can read through reviews on review sites. You can search for Facebook groups of people you think might offer or buy the product/service you are offering. In those groups you can ask for feedback on your idea, or even better, if anyone would be willing to test your product or service in exchange for their honest feedback. "Ask and you shall receive." If you don't ask, you will never know.

Regarding conducting general market research, you are ultimately trying to discover:

- what customers like, what they don't like, what puts them off, what makes them excited, what they wish they could find, what frustrates them, what they are willing to pay, what they value

- which competitors are doing well and which ones aren't (and if can you see why)

- if there any new trends in the market

- if there is room to bring any of your personality, skills, and experience into the offering to make yourself stand out from the competition

Have a Professional Review Your Plan

If you have pulled together most of the above plan but are still struggling to work out your budget, and your forecasted profit and loss, cash flow, balance sheet or breakeven figures, I strongly recommend getting a professional to look at it for you. Or at least invest in yourself with education to learn what the figures mean and what you need to know. You need to have a good handle on the numbers when you start, or you risk losing it all unnecessarily. Top tip here: if you plan on showing your business plan to a potential investor or getting financial advice on your figures, book that appointment now—you have just given yourself a strict deadline and the motivation you need to get your plan finished.

Start Simple

You can always add more layers to your business later. We could have easily looked at all the other campsites out there and said, "ooh they have caravan pitches, campervan pitches, tent pitches, bell tents, pods, a play park, a swimming pool, a tarmac car park, a café, and a reception area at the entrance, we ought to do that too". Had we gone down that route, I assure you, I would be balder than a coot right now.

It would have required a huge upfront investment to start where we wanted to end up; heavy borrowing as we didn't have the money, high running costs, a long set-up time, and an immediate need to hire staff to maintain and run all these facilities. At the time, I had only had experience managing a team of a handful of builders, all of whom were self-employed, so I had no knowledge of the intricacies and the legalities of employing people. I had no knowledge of swimming pools. I had limited time to put into building a business as I was already working on other projects. I had no desire to borrow a huge amount of money upfront. And I also had no desire to turn our lovely little peaceful farm into a highly-manicured, commercial, impersonal campsite.

I wanted to start simple. I wanted to grow it organically—reinvesting each year what we had made so that we didn't have the pressure of borrowing and having to meet interest payments each month. I wanted to create a space that people would love and that I would enjoy working in. And I wanted to start as soon as I could. So, I decided that we would start with the basics on our site and then adjust our strategy as we went, according to what extras we wanted to offer.

Now, I'm not saying this is the right path for everyone. Some of you will want to speed it along, and borrowing money is the fastest way to do that. But I do recommend that whatever your end goal is, scale it back to the simplest version to start. This will ensure that you get the foundations right at the start. You will figure out the problems early on and solve them before they become too costly. You will get a better idea of exactly what direction you want to go with your business and what you want to offer. You will learn what things you enjoy the most and what you want to change. While things are simple and small at the beginning, it is much easier to tweak and refine. Focus on one key product or service at the beginning and you will make your life so much easier. You can always build upon it, adding in extras once you know you can manage it. There is also the research conducted by Barry Schwartz about the Paradox of Choice—where eliminating consumer choices can greatly reduce anxiety for shoppers. So, if your chosen first business is a café, despite what you might intuitively think, a simpler menu with just six choices will be much easier for your consumers than if you are offering 36 meal options. And the benefit for you is that it is much simpler for you to learn how to get the product right each time, easier to analyze the exact process behind delivering that product (it is essential to figure this out—from marketing your product to the consumer having the product), and easier to get feedback and tweak to suit.

Another point to make here is that while you should set up your business according to your local and regional government's legislation and regulations (depending upon where you are in the world and what you will be doing, you may need to register as a particular legal entity or have certain structures in place before you start doing business), my advice is still to keep your company structure as simple as possible at the beginning. A lot of new entrepreneurs rush into setting up as a limited company (LC) right at the very start (and often before they have even nailed their strategy) because they think it shows they are a 'real' business, when in reality there may have been better options available regarding accounting, tax, and flexibility for their particular business. An LC is not the only type of legitimate business designation available. If you are unfamiliar with what the different business setups are, seek professional legal advice to help explain the differences. And make sure that you have looked into the various insurances you might need to cover yourself in the case of a problem further down the line. Having some legal protection in place (whether it be through company structure or insurance) offer more benefits than they typically cost. The peace of mind that comes with it—that if things do go wrong, you and your family won't lose everything you have ever worked for—means you won't shy away from opportunities that may stretch you, and require you to grow. This goes double for my overarching advice to start simple, the peace of mind you have by knowing you can handle what is on your plate gives you the confidence to stretch beyond and grow your business properly.

Research Your Competition

A quick note here on competition—although most people think that competition is a bad thing, I advocate the opposite. If there are already competitors in your market, chances are you're on to a good thing. It means there is a market for what you can offer. You likely will not come up with a brand new, out-of-this-world idea. You can always inject some of your personality into what you offer that will make it stand out from the rest or find a slightly underserved section of the market that you could serve well. Don't assume that just because someone else was there first, they will get all of the market share. So do your research but don't allow yourself to get disheartened by the fact that someone else is ahead of you, doing something similar.

Commit to Your Business Fully

If you have tested your market, are enjoying the process, and think you could (for the most part) enjoy delivering that product or service and running that business, then commit to the idea fully.

Committing to trying your business is one thing, committing to doing all you can to make it work is another. I truly believe that if you embrace the phrase "Where there's a will, there's a way", it will serve you well. Because you will undoubtedly find excuses for why others can do what you can't. The opportunities they have and you don't. This isn't useful thinking, it's self-pity. If you want something, figure out a way to get it. And maybe that means accepting that you can't have it all now, that you have to work your way up to having that business. Maybe that means starting this business as a side business alongside your full time job and growing it slowly to the point where you can then step away. Maybe that means figuring out your personal survival budget and getting a part time job to cover those costs, while you put everything else you have into the new business. **If you believe you can do it, you will find a way to do it.** You just need to find an inroad you can start at. You can always change course as you learn more, gain more contacts, and build your pot of money. This is exactly the route we took and it can be yours too!

Have an Exit Strategy

If you aren't 100% sure, however, that it will be your passion business or your only business, there is something I strongly advise you take time to think about before you commit. Formulate a back-up plan or an exit strategy. This is in case you decide you don't want to run it any more or the business fails. How are you going to get out of it? What are you prepared to lose?

Now, I'm not talking about having a back-up plan that means you won't commit. I do like the 'all in' analogy of burning your ships so that you do your best to make it a success. But I'm also not about throwing away your life savings on a whim of an idea. I am all about creating the life and business you love without sacrificing one for the other. So if you find you start something and you genuinely decide there is no part of it that is engaging or interesting to you, and you can't tweak it to make it suit your lifestyle and what you want, it is far better for your own emotional wellbeing to know that it's ok, feel proud that you tried, and feel comfortable stepping away and going back to the drawing board to try something else. Having a back-up plan allows you to do this safely, without losing everything you've built outside of this one idea.

This is why I think you should do your research well, decide what you are committed to investing, consider the worst-case scenario, and make peace with it. For example, worst case is that I put in 50% of my savings, give it a go, I decide I hate it, and I let it go. At the end of the day I've lost half of my savings, but I have decided what I don't want, improved my business skills, I have some savings left over, and I'm one step closer to figuring out and deciding what I do want to do.

Your exit strategy could also be one that serves you in the future, even if the business is working, if you decide you don't want to continue with running it, you can sell it and be paid a percentage of the profits going forward. Having this plan will make it so much easier to have a go in the first place, knowing that whatever you step into won't be a jail sentence for the rest of your life. It's so much more empowering to know that you have options if this current idea doesn't give you the lifestyle you want. All the skills you learn from this first attempt (call it your practice business) will be transferrable to the next one—one step closer to your true calling—so nothing is wasted.

Learn As You Go

It is important not to let the fact that you don't know everything hold you back. There will always be more to learn. You can always improve. There is no end point. Learn the foundations (see chapter 4), commit to ongoing learning throughout your business journey, and then get going. **Typically, humans learn best by doing.**

Now, granted, for some businesses, you may legally need to have specific qualifications/skills before you are able to start. But in general, running a business involves so many skillsets and knowledge, to wait until you are an expert with the highest possible level of education would mean that no business would ever get started. Instead, you need to start where you are. Start before you are ready and then figure it out along the way. In the words of Napoleon Hill, "Start where you stand, and work whatever tools you may have at your command and better tools will be found as you go along."

A quick note here for if you do need to do a particular qualification to get started—sign up for that course now, while you are motivated, and set a date to open your doors as soon as you are qualified.

Allow Yourself to Be a Beginner

I go into this in more detail in the mindset chapter, but I want to touch on it here first. Make it a priority to work on your beginner mindset. What this means is to go into this adventure accepting that you are a beginner and that you might make mistakes. Perfectionism has no place in the entrepreneurial world. While it is always nice to do a perfect job, if you don't allow yourself to put your work out there before you feel like it is perfect, the world will never end up seeing it. I thoroughly recommend repeating the mantra, "Done is better than perfect". Allow yourself to be a beginner.

Adopting a beginner mindset will make it so much easier to start in the beginning. If you think you should have it all together before you start, you will never start because the truth is that no one has it all together—even if it looks like it from the outside. Be yourself, be honest, do what's right, and be compassionate with yourself when you put yourself and your product or service out there. Maybe it won't be received well. Don't take it personally. You didn't know. You are just a beginner. Ask how you could have made it better. Ask what they would have wanted instead. Being open to trying new things along the way and having an open mind for learning is what owning a business is all about—trial and error, trying new things, seeing what works, seeing what doesn't, and tweaking your product or service to meet the evolving needs of the market and your customers.

Action Prompts

- Decide if becoming a business owner is for you (know the upsides and downsides)

- Undertake the Seven Levels Deep Exercise and figure out your 'why'

- Question your objections behind why you haven't started yet (i.e. Call all out your B.S. excuses) and draw a line in the sand

- Latch on to your new reasons for starting now

- When considering your business idea:

  o Use the internet to assess the marketplace and trends around a handful of ideas

  o Assess your strengths and weaknesses, experiences and skills

  o Analyze whether you think you could deliver the product or service well

  o Assess the opportunities you have available to you and any assets you might have

  o Consider the lifestyle you want and whether or not this business could deliver it

  o Consider the timing of your launch and existing trends in the market

- o Find competitors offering something similar and buy from them

- o Conduct market research into these competitors and your potential customers

- o Work out what else you could bring to the table that would differentiate you

- Assess and validate your potential idea thoroughly

- Make a concise, snappy business plan that leaves room to grow, but covers the key areas and set a deadline for getting all things in place for starting your business soon

- Figure out if you need extra training before you are able to start and sign up for it promptly

- Work out how to keep your business model simple and build protections into it

- Decide on an opening/launch date

- Map out your exit strategy

- Work on your beginner mindset

- Actively decide that you are willing to find a way to make it work

- **Commit yourself fully**

CHAPTER 2
MARKETING YOUR BUSINESS

I'm not sure where the phrase "if you build it, they will come" came from, but I subscribed to it pretty well. And we got lucky—I put a single ad up that cost me £50 (approximately $60 US) on one glamping directory that I found within minutes of searching Google, and we had our first customer booked in two days later. Then another customer found us and booked with us, and then another and another. And I thought to myself, *Well this is easy, the saying must be true!*

I was wrong. We got lucky early on. The glamping directory I stumbled upon, at the time, was doing very well on the Google home page—it was right near the top. They must have spent a lot that year on their SEO (Search Engine Optimization). And as we caught the trend of glamping fairly early on, there were only a handful of glamping sites in our area, so we were on their first page when a customer came to search for a site in our county. On top of that, we were small, so we had only a single tent to fill, and even as we expanded that summer to have three tents, we needed only a handful of customers at a time to fill our spaces.

The following year however, I expanded again (adding another four tents to our site), set our open date for early in the year and, having signed up to a whole extra **one** glamping directory, thought we would once again be able to fill our spots with no issue. And this is when I noticed the quiet periods. We had a lot of last-minute bookings, the weekends were mostly full, and we had some longer stays during the busy summer holidays, but the shoulders of the season and midweek dates were deathly quiet. I assumed it must be because our service wasn't good enough. So, we added more quirky things to the site. We installed shelters so our guests could have dry space to eat under when it rained, we added a child's swing, we changed out the mattresses for more comfy ones, we added games to the site, and replaced things that were starting to look tatty. And we still struggled to get booked out. I still hadn't worked out that it might be the marketing.

Looking back, I can see how obvious it was. But it's a very different story when you are in the middle of running the business and focusing on each day, one at a time, on delivering the best service you can, and not thinking how, even though the marketing worked last year, it may not have been working so well this year.

Fortunately, by the third year, I had listed our campsite in a dozen more places, we had an SEO professional tweak our own website which took it to page one of Google, I had figured out which customers to target, and I posted more regularly and consistently on two different social media platforms. And so, while the shoulders of the season were still much slower than the high peak season of the school summer holidays, we did have considerably more bookings than that second year. Because I was finally marketing our business!

* * *

Your Marketing Strategy

The key takeaway from our own experience is that **marketing is fundamental to a successful business**. Do not treat it like an afterthought. If you absolutely don't want to learn marketing yourself, then pay for it. Just don't neglect it. There is no point putting your heart and soul into the rest of your business, creating an amazing product or service, and then having no customers because they don't know you even exist. Doing sporadic bits of random marketing and hoping that it works, that the customers you do get will tell others about you, will be a super slow and painful route. It will be hard to plan for every single other aspect of your business, it won't be scalable, and you are likely to lose faith and momentum, if that is the sum total of your marketing. Building an amazing product or service as the first step. The second step is to market your business like crazy.

The options you have available to you to market your business are now endless. You can still go the traditional route of billboards, newspapers, and physical magazines, but now thanks to the digital age, there are heaps more ways available that you can use, many of which are free. We'll talk more about the different types later in the chapter. You can use as many or as little as you like. And this is where most new business owners go wrong. They think that putting adverts out in as many mediums as they can is what their marketing strategy is about. They jump into which medium they are going to use, basing it purely on a hunch, writing a sales pitch for what they do, and take little to no time in getting the foundations right first. Taking the time to figure out a proper marketing strategy will make all the difference in your business success. Your marketing strategy is the overall strategy you will use to tell your potential clients and customers who you are and educate them on why they should choose you over your competitors. It should comprise:

- What results you are selling (the transformation)

- Who you are selling it to (your niche and ideal client)

- How you are speaking to your customers (your messaging)

- What types of things you will be telling your customers (your content)

- How you will get your customer to buy (your conversions)

- How you will get your messages to your customers (your mediums)

- How you will measure your marketing efforts (tracking and objectives)

The Transformation

The absolute first thing to do when figuring out your marketing strategy is to make sure that you are crystal clear on what the product or service is that you are selling (this should be informed by your market research, testing, and validating process). This may seem obvious, but so many people skip this part. You have to go a little bit deeper here to consider why anyone would actually buy what you are selling. What I mean by that, is what *results* will they be buying. **People tend to buy things because of how they think they will feel when they have purchased it**, i.e. they think about the result that the thing will bring them, how this will make them feel. This results from millions of years of evolution of our brains. Our brains have evolved to drive us to take action that either maximizes pleasure or minimizes pain. So, every single thing we buy is motivated by this. And the clearer the results/outcome shows how it will make us feel (by either minimizing pain or maximizing pleasure), the easier it will be to convert the sale.

For example, you could try to sell "16 round white dissolvable tablets with a chemical composition that inhibits sensory receptors" or you could sell "pain relief tablets". People are buying the results or the outcome. They are buying the transformation from being uncomfortable and in pain to being comfortable and pain free. You could sell "factory-made hard solid shapes of rubber you can bounce and pull and not damage" or you could sell "virtually indestructible dog toys for endless play time and connection with your furry friend". You can sell "a room on a ship" or you can sell "a dream vacation".

Now, you may be thinking this is just semantics—and, fair enough, I am just talking about messaging. But sitting down and focusing on why your customer would want or need your product/service, what exact results it can offer, and what problems they may have that your product or service solves (i.e. their pain points) won't only help with the messaging in your sales pitches, but it will help you figure out exactly who your ideal customer is. This will help you figure out where they will be, how to speak to them, and how to ultimately convert them into buying customers.

The easiest way to do this is brainstorm all the things your product/service does, how it helps, what results it enables, and what emotional pain points/desires it solves.

Once you have a clear idea of what exactly you sell and are able to connect the intangible results they will get to your product or service, you can create much more effective messaging for marketing it. And if you get to this point and realize that you are struggling to connect the results the customer is buying with your product/service, now is the time to tweak it slightly so you can.

Your Niche and Ideal Client

The next most important thing to work out in your marketing strategy is exactly who it is you are targeting with your product or service (i.e. what group of people are you aiming to sell to). The two concepts most frequently used to describe the 'who' are your 'niche' and your 'ideal client'. There is some overlap between the two, but here's how I like to define them. Your niche is the group of people, as a collective, that you are targeting (e.g. stay-at-home mothers, female entrepreneurs, online retail businesses). The ideal client concept is to think of an individual within that group that would be a perfect fit for your product or service with regard to their struggles and aspirations (e.g. a mother who is aspiring to start their first business and doesn't know where to start). One reason why you want to pick a particular group of people to sell to is so that you know where to focus your efforts because in knowing who they are, you can work out where they hang out. Another reason is because you will have a better idea of what to say in your marketing if you know who you are talking to. I'll go into this in more detail later, but first I want to talk about the process of 'nailing your niche' (i.e. picking the particular customer group you want to serve).

One of the biggest barriers to nailing your niche is not the challenge itself of figuring out who your niche could be, but a reluctance to make the niche too small. This is one of the hardest things in business to get your head around and it is the one part of marketing that most people resist, because by purposefully excluding customers, they think it will inevitably mean they will be missing out on potential sales. But as the saying goes, "If you are trying to speak to everyone, you are speaking to no one". **You simply cannot appeal to every single person** and in trying to, you will blend into a sea of similar options and spend way more than you want to on marketing because you will be paying (either with money or time) to be everywhere to find everyone. Trust that even in a smaller group of people, there are plenty of potential customers/clients—and trust that you are much more likely to find them because you know who they are and where to look for them.

One technique that can be particularly effective in narrowing down who your ideal client is, is to create an ideal client avatar. This is where you visualize in your head one person that your product/service would be perfect for—what they do for a job, where they live, how old they are, what their biggest fears are, what their objections to buying would be…etc.—and write it all down as a sort of character description of this ideal client you seek. If you write down 100 things about your ideal client avatar, you will end up with a very clear idea of who that client is, and inevitably what your larger clientele would look like. Another way to come up with your ideal client avatar is to think of a person who you enjoyed working with before or a person who acts in accordance with your values and model your niche on that. You can then use this information to better reach, market, and engage with them, ultimately building a lasting relationship.

Some business coaches would counter this advice and say preference should have nothing to do with it. If they want to buy from you, let them, they will say. But I disagree. Loving your customers and wanting to provide the best possible product/service and greatest value to them is so much easier when you enjoy working with those types of people. This is particularly important when your product or service requires a lot of direct interaction with that customer, over an extended period. You might not find it easy to get along with everybody. And that's ok. Provided you are not discriminating unfairly, you can decide that your niche is based on someone who you have liked working with previously. We all have the freedom in life to decide what and who we like and what and who we don't like. And if you have committed to this journey in your life, the challenges you will face, just in starting and growing your business, will be hard enough without adding on an extra layer of having to work with people you don't naturally click with or aren't that compatible with your product or service. One phrase I particularly like when referring to your marketing and your ideal client is, **"Marketing is about attracting the customers you want and repelling the ones you don't"**. I love this, because there are some customers you do not want. For example, our campsite is an eco-campsite due to our own values regarding caring for the environment, so we decided we wanted to attract customers with similar values as it means that they are more likely to recycle their rubbish and take care of the environment we are sharing with them.

In accordance with this, it is important that your marketing communicates who your product or service is for effectively, to save you wasting money and time explaining to a customer that what you offer isn't right for them (e.g. that you offer counseling to teenagers, not 40 year old's).

Figuring out your niche will help you figure out what makes you stand out from your competition. This is typically referred to as your Unique Selling Point (USP). Considering your niche and your USP simultaneously is one of the most helpful things you can do when figuring out the direction your business will take. You will have hopefully already thought about this when conducting your initial market research into the idea and the competition, but when you think about who your niche is and you try to narrow it down to a specific group of people, sometimes additional ideas come out that will help you stand out even further.

Perhaps, you could instead market yourselves so you are targeting a new segment of the market, that would benefit from your product or service. Perhaps if you tweaked your product or service just slightly, it would benefit to a different sector of the market than who your competition is targeting. For example, if your idea is to make and sell Journals, you will be competing with a huge number of much bigger organizations that are already on the shelves of many shops. If, however, you narrow this niche down to mothers instead of just anybody, you can think about why mothers would benefit from having a journal (e.g. to help ensure that they are taking time for themselves each day to organize their day and the extra-curricular activities their kids are doing, reflect, practice gratitude and plan for the next day). If you then narrow it down further to mothers with young children, you can now see all the additional problems this group of women will have in finding alone time to fill such a journal. And this is where you can spot a potential opportunity— perhaps by pairing up the mother's journal with a kid's journal or a matching coloring book that you could market both to the mother as a way of creating quality quiet time alongside her small children, while she gets some space to organize her mind. And just like that, you have distinguished yourself from the competition (you have your USP), you have found your people, you can picture their problems, their objections to buying, you can create a link between your product and the results you are selling, you can figure out where you can find them, and you have figured out some of your messaging already.

If you have narrowed down to a group of customers that would particularly benefit from your product or service, but you still don't think you are standing out from your competition, try to figure out a way in which you could add a slight difference to your product or service to make it stand out. If you are your own brand (for instance, if you are an event planner) then **you will be that key difference**. By bringing your personality into your branding and your experience, you and your story could be the reason you stand out from the competition.

Your Messaging

Having worked out your niche and your ideal client, you should now have a good idea of who you are selling to, what they want, and how your unique product/service (combined with your personality, experience, and skills) will give them the results/transformation and, more importantly, the feeling they are after. The next thing to consider is your messaging. It needs to be consistent across all platforms, your ads, and your branding. It needs to be clear. And it needs to hook your ideal client in and repel the rest. After all, you don't want someone to pick up your product and be disappointed that it wasn't what they expected. Marketing your USP clearly through your messaging (particularly where it might deter the clients who aren't looking for that specific thing), will help make sure your clients know exactly what they are getting.

You are looking to use messaging to accurately describe your product/service, the benefits, and the outcomes your customer is looking for. You can use messaging to speak directly to your ideal client by using phrases or questions they identify with. And you can use directly searchable keywords in your messaging that will help your ideal customer find you and your product/service.

The easiest way to ensure that you are doing all of these is to take time before you start marketing to create an 'elevator pitch' and some key phrases and terms that relate to your product or service. An 'elevator pitch' is a sentence or two that summarizes your business/product/ service that could (as the name implies) be delivered in the average time it takes to complete an elevator ride. You can typically include your ideal client, what they struggle with (their problem/solution), what your product/service or business is about, and how it can bring your client the results they are after. You also want to pull out any keywords that are being repeatedly used to describe your product/service from your interactions with your market research customers and any other work or research you have been doing. This includes the pain points that frequently come up and frequently used words describing the result or transformation that your product or service provides. The longer you take brainstorming about your ideal client and speaking to your ideal clients about the pain points they have, the results they want, and the key words they use to describe themselves, the better your messaging will be at speaking to and attracting your ideal customer.

We realized the importance of using the same language as your ideal clients when we realized that the words we were using to describe our campsite were invoking a different image in our customers' minds than in ours. For example, some customers immediately linked the word 'retreat' to yoga, spirituality, religion, and health, while other customers linked it to business coaching and writing. In our eyes, it was just a nicer way to say accommodation or a place to escape to for a holiday. The importance of using your customers' language then becomes so easy to see. You can use similar variations of your key message across several platforms and be secure in the knowledge that you are portraying your business product or service consistently to the right people, in a way that is likely to work.

By having generic messaging that doesn't sell you, or your USP, and doesn't speak out to your ideal customer, you likely won't stand out. For example, if you have a café that sells tasty dishes and is aiming to serve anybody and everybody, chances are if your online messaging is something like, "Lovely café, come try it out!" you won't stand out from the other 20 cafes in the same town, and your customer is also not going to know what to expect when they get there (maybe it is a greasy spoon café, or a café that sells only hot drinks and cakes, or a café that sells pre-prepared sandwiches only, or a café that does full lunches, or a vegan café—you get the gist). Contrast this with a café deciding they will only serve homemade, healthy, wholesome vegan dishes and that they are dog-friendly. They are not only going to instantly stand out from the rest of the cafes, but they will speak directly to the vegan dog-owner who wants to eat something delicious, healthy, and vegan for lunch, while out on a stroll with their dog. This café would be the perfect place. They might not even consider going to the other cafes because of the hassle of asking whether or not they are dog-friendly and if they have vegan dishes.

The above example illustrates the key point of attracting your ideal client and repelling those who wouldn't benefit from your business anyway. You can also tailor your messaging to hook in your ideal client. For example, you could use the tag line, "Do you fancy the most delicious vegan lunch today, on your way back from walking your dog?" This would instantly hook someone in who is hungry, a vegan, and has a dog. It's much harder to do that with a generic café. "Are you hungry for a tasty lunch?" See the difference? Nothing stands out. And maybe it does attract the vegan with the dog, but then they realize the café is not dog-friendly. Not ideal—a complete waste of a customer interaction. So, although it may seem like the limited number of vegans in an area would restrict how many customers you could have, the chances are if you have done your research and have seen the growing trend toward healthy eating, healthier lifestyles, and tasty vegan foods, you can gauge whether your niche is too small, or if you will still attract customers who want to try vegan food in their diet, without becoming 100% vegan.

Trust me on this one. Knowing your niche well means you can utilize specific language to create clear and consistent messaging to let your dream clients know that you are the perfect fit for them. And you can tailor your selling and design process to speak directly to your ideal client's interests and values. Your marketing and messaging will then become much more effective and much easier for you to manage, once you have nailed down exactly who you are talking to and what you can offer.

Your Content

It is important to note here that despite the main objective of marketing being to ultimately sell your product or service, the majority of your marketing will not be sales pitches. Instead, it should be a mixture of 'awareness' content and 'consideration' content. These are designed with your client's buying journey in mind. The client first needs to know you exist and appreciate that you know what you are talking about, before even considering looking into buying from you.

Awareness content educates your ideal client with either general data, insights, or research that they are seeking for a particular problem they have (letting them know you exist in the process). Blogs, podcasts, informative tips on a social media post and lead magnets are good examples of providing value to the customer on a problem they have, while letting them know you exist. The idea is that the customer stumbles upon your blog or link to your lead magnet (a free piece of valuable information you give in exchange for the customer's email address) through searching for the solution to their problem, and both can also demonstrate that you have expertise on the matter and could be of service to them. The other advantage of these types of content is that they can be offered to other businesses with a similar ideal client (but who aren't directly competing) as a way of collaboration through providing free value to their existing audience, while also getting you in front of potential future clients. Often, if they like what you share, clients from that audience will pay attention to the other things you are doing, so you are not only able to gain credibility in your field as the 'expert' but you will also grow your audience.

Consideration Content, on the other hand, is where you focus on creating content that explains your *specific* product/service in detail, how you can help your ideal client with their problem, and what is different about your business to everyone else's (i.e. your USP). Examples of this content include videos of testimonials from previous clients or customers, an Instagram story of what the process is like working with you, helpful tips on how to use your product or service, posts on the features of your product or service (in our case a Facebook post that lists what we provide to our guests in our accommodation), and price lists. You can combine the two types by adding in how to find you, what you are selling, or a story about why you can teach the lesson you just taught. Besides these, if you are willing to overdeliver on the value you give and you add your personality, some social fun, and emotive posts into your marketing, and you embrace stepping in to being the 'face' of your brand as the owner, you are much more likely to be remembered when the client is ready to buy.

Examples of what you could share or write about, that will mean that your audience remembers you and gets to know the 'you' behind the business could simply be telling a funny or interesting story about something that happened to you, or a story about why you got into business in the first place, sharing insights you now have.

This is usually where business owners pull back into their shells, as they either don't want to show their personality in the business (for fear they will come across as unprofessional) or they don't want to actually show their face as the brand owner (possibly due to visibility fears, or a feeling that it isn't important). This will cost them more customers than they will ever realize because even though marketing tactics have changed, the root of marketing has always been trust and familiarity. **People**

want to buy from people, from a brand they know, like, and trust. Customers typically connect their desires, values, and aspirations to a brand. And regardless of the size of the business, or what you do, you are essentially your brand. So when you put content out there that shows you and your values and you can connect with the audience authentically, on an emotional level, your customers will much more easily build up the 'know, like, and trust' relationship with you and your product/service, increasing their likelihood of buying.

Companies who fail to recognize this have to ultimately work way harder and pay more for marketing than the rest to develop that 'know, like, and trust' factor, as brand personality is much harder to show in impersonal messaging. Now, this doesn't mean you have to share all aspects of your personal life, things that would compromise your security, or things you are uncomfortable with sharing. You can filter and edit what you share. It will come across as more authentic if you stay true to your personal values, rather than making up what you think the customer will want to hear. You can still curate the personality that you want to show while remaining authentic.

If you aren't shy though, if you are willing to put your face out there as part of your business' brand identity and you are raw, honest, vulnerable, and authentically you, you will find that you will capture a much more loyal audience, much more quickly.

The dietary supplement company Your Superfoods is a prime example. The couple who started it are very much the face of their brand—they tell their raw, honest, heartfelt story about the boyfriend's story of recovering from cancer and the reason their product came into existence. They quickly built a following on social media and raised their brand profile to global levels, forming a relationship with their audience by showing vulnerability and frequently connecting through engaging directly with their audience.

The key takeaways here are to be yourself, engage on an emotional level with your audience, and then nurture your audience by consistently showing up, engaging as a person, and delivering value. This doesn't even have to be by just creating and posting your own content either. Social media especially provides a great opportunity to add value and build relationships with your ideal client by simply interacting with them and using your expertise to solve their problems. By doing this, you are offering awareness content and building up that relationship. Statistics regarding how long it takes to build that relationship with your customers before they are ready to buy from you vary, but one that is frequently tossed around is that they need to hear from you up to 27 times in order to have built up that 'know, like, and trust' factor enough. So, the quicker you can make that emotional connection with your audience, the better.

Contrary to what a lot of new entrepreneurs think, branding is less about logos and names, and more about the values you stand by, how you want your customers to feel when they perceive you and interact with you, and what you want your customers to remember you by. It's the emotion behind what someone feels, sees, and experiences when they interact with your business on any level. The overall personality of your brand is more important than your logo or name in the early stages, because your brand personality is what attracts and keeps your customers. So this is what needs to come through in your messaging.

Converting Leads to Sales

It is also important to know a little bit about consumer psychology and buying behavior when starting out, as this will help you get your messaging to be even more effective in actually converting leads to sales. It isn't enough to just attract who you want and repel those you don't. You want to make sure that your messaging is speaking directly to your ideal client and that they are listening for more. The structure that works most effectively for this is the 'hook-story-close' method.

Essentially, you start your messaging with a direct question that grabs the attention of your potential customer (i.e. the hook). You will have more than likely seen it used in ads and on websites, and now that you know it, you will probably notice it more and more. A hook is one of those common questions we hear at the beginning of advertisements, "Are you struggling with 'x'?", "Do you wish you had 'x'?", "Are you fed up with scanning the menu for vegan dishes?", "Are you tired of asking cafes if they welcome dogs?". The hook gets you interested because you relate to it instantly, particularly if it invokes an emotion.

The second part of the method is to tell a story. People love stories. They are far more engaging than just plain facts. They can often relate to stories, even if it isn't their story exactly. The story can be of your product or service, the story of you and your opinion, struggles that are related to the hook somehow, or the story of a customer who has bought from you in the past and their transformation. But be enthusiastic. You are aiming to persuade them with your enthusiasm for the results that your product or service can deliver. This is where picking a business or product/service that you are super passionate about will pay dividends. It doesn't have to be your one and only passion. But **profit follows passion**, one of my coaches, Lisa Johnson, often says. It is easy to be enthusiastic about your product if you love it, but even if you don't, you can be enthusiastic about the results it can deliver.

The third part of the method is to either ask for the sale or ask for some level of interaction that requires effort by the customer (i.e. a call to action). If you have done a good job at part one and two, are speaking to the right person, and engaging and persuading them with a relatable story, the third part will be much easier. When actually selling, you can leverage the fear of missing out (FOMO) phenomenon by giving an incentive to buy now—either by way of a discount/bonus if they act quickly, or by giving a deadline or alluding to the fact that numbers/ places are limited and running out. You will see this time and time again. It's used by hundreds of companies worldwide, which is proof it works.

Getting someone to take some action is an important first step in their customer journey with you. It is much easier to get them to interact again and again if they have already interacted once. You are in essence, building up a relationship with them. And this is a key point to note here. **You need to work on building a relationship with your customer before they buy from you**. As I mentioned earlier, people tend to buy only once they have decided that they know, like, and trust you. And this is where the majority of your marketing efforts will go— into building awareness of you and your brand and building relationships before you even get to the point where you are asking for the sale.

Many people struggle with asking for the sale and simply don't bother. But you need to push through the discomfort or you will not survive in business. One reason for this is that they see selling as a sleazy approach to getting someone's money. If this resonates with you, you need to consciously work on changing how you see selling. The easiest way to do this by far is to understand the results your product or service offers and the pain point it solves. This will help show you why your service or product is valuable, and when you truly believe that it is valuable, you will have a much easier time putting a value on it to sell it. **You also need to realize that if you don't sell them your product or service, someone else will.** If you are at all competitive, this should help with your motivation levels somewhat. If it doesn't, but you actually do care about serving people on a deeper level, think about the fact that the customers who are buying elsewhere may be buying an inferior product or service to what they could get from you. That motivates me for sure.

If you still feel uncomfortable, take marketing and sales courses to improve your skills and work with a mindset coach on your thoughts around selling. This is an investment you will easily be able to make back in your sales afterwards.

Not only should you learn to be comfortable with asking for the sale however, you should also work on becoming comfortable asking for referrals and testimonials/reviews. It will save you so much money if you get referrals and repeat customers, rather than having to go out each time and get new ones.

Your Mediums

GENERAL POINTS TO CONSIDER

The first thing to consider when selecting the mediums you will be using to market your business is where your ideal client is likely to hang out. This is usually made much easier by having done the work to figure out who it is that you are targeting. For example, if you are selling services to businesses or corporate professionals, LinkedIn should be a consideration. In contrast to this, if you are selling handmade baby clothes to mothers, Facebook groups where you know mothers will be would be a better option. Often people get hung up at this stage because they don't know intuitively where their ideal client will be, so they take a random guess to decide. The better way to do this is to actually put some time into researching where they might be—Google various search terms about your customer and what you think they might be interested in, and see what comes up. Type into the Facebook and Instagram search functions 'mom/mum groups' if you are searching for mothers and see what comes up. Ask your friends and family for ideas. Look for your competitors and see how they are marketing to their clients. Ask your competitor's customers how they usually find their supplier. Get some ideas, then test them. If you don't ask, you don't get. Just don't overcomplicate it.

The second thing to consider is the cost of the options available and your own marketing budget. **Yes, you will need a budget set aside just for marketing. Set this up at the start.** This will make you much more diligent in assessing what does and doesn't work (I'll go into more detail on this later on). But mostly it will mean that you take your marketing strategy seriously and will force you to focus your efforts in a few areas, rather than trying to be everywhere at all once. It will also stop you falling for spontaneous and usually bad deals from cold callers—as I did (a glamping directory I had never heard of that only comes up on Google if you type their exact name in, rather than any key search terms).

Regarding the cost of the mediums, social media platforms are great places to test the market and grow organically, for free. But paid directories or adverts might get you there quicker. I always recommend trying to minimize marketing costs early on, at least until you are 100% sure about who your ideal client is and are confident that your messaging is in the right place and attracting them. Once you know you have a system that is working to generate leads/customers for you, then you can scale it up and put more money into it.

WEBSITES

If your business needs a website, then I recommend learning the basics and creating it yourself initially. As your business grows and you need more complicated things added, you can hire help at that point. There are lots of great website templates out there that are free or low cost and easy to master to start with. If you can choose a website platform that you can expand upon later easily, rather than needing to rebuild the whole thing from scratch, all the better. Have some vision in mind as to what your website and business could grow to be, but don't get too hung up on it if this will stop you from taking action altogether. It is better to start with something low cost and simple initially, until you are making consistent income and you know what you are doing is working.

The reason I recommend doing the website yourself if you can is that if you hire someone else to build your website from scratch, not only will you have a big expenditure up front, but often website designers will hook you in to a monthly payment plan on their favorite hosting platform (which might not be that economical for you). It might also mean that if you want to make simple changes, you become dependent upon the designer to implement these, so it can quickly become expensive and inflexible to maintain.

Another great reason I see for deciding to learn the basics for simple things like this is that learning how to do hard things produces incredible character-building skills in yourself, which will undoubtedly serve you in other areas. And as your business grows and you find that you like what you are doing and want to scale further, or the platform and simple website you built initially no longer works, you can use money and content you have made from within the business to then pay and instruct someone externally to upgrade it for you. You will also have a much better idea of what exactly you are asking for at this point, and you will be able to tell if they are trying to pull the wool over your eyes with the amount of work involved and the quotation given.

Another good tip here is that having links to your own website or social media account pages on other peoples' websites and directories will help boost your placement on various search engines. In addition, there are a multitude of other tricks you can do on your own website to optimize it for being found (namely, SEO). For example, writing and posting blogs regularly that are linked to your website, keeping your content and images current by editing it frequently, and adding the right search tags. If you don't know SEO, either learn about it promptly or hire an expert.

THIRD-PARTY WEBSITES

If your product or service could be sold on a third-party website (perhaps a booking platform or a virtual shop like Etsy), you will need to weigh the advantages and disadvantages associated. It could get you greater market reach, and more customers initially before your brand gets established, but you will likely pay either upfront payments or payments on commission for what gets sold (or both sometimes). Often, however, customers will find you on a more widely known third-party site and then seek you out directly (sometimes you are permitted to list your website on their listing page), so this can be a good way to gain marketing exposure without it costing you much. Thus, I do recommend in the early stages allocating at least a small portion of your products/service to be marketed this way, particularly if the upfront costs are low and you only pay on commission (so you only pay out if you actually get the sale), as it helps cash flow in the early years and also boosts your SEO. Limiting the numbers available on the third-party site also means you won't be losing all potential direct customers to this indirect route.

SOCIAL MEDIA PLATFORMS AND OTHER MEDIUMS

If you decide upon a social media platform, figure out how to use it to your advantage, but do not rely on beating the algorithm. First, it changes all the time. Second, the time and effort spent in trying to figure it out would be better spent either by investing in marketing you know works or by learning how to create high-quality, emotive, engaging content that is consistent with your brand, your values, and your personality, and that is valuable to the customer (not just descriptions and photos of your product/service and other sales posts). If your content is resonating with your customer, or even if they are just enjoying it for entertainment, they will be more likely to engage with it, follow your posts, and interact with you more, so will stay on the platform for longer (which is what the algorithm is aiming to achieve—thus, it will reward you for it by expanding your reach on that platform). Remember, it is all about building that 'know, like, and trust' factor and building relationships with your customers in advance.

Another useful point to consider here is the effectiveness of the type of messaging you are using on each platform. For example, trends currently show that video is much more effective at grabbing people's attention on social media at the moment, which makes perfect sense when you consider how much noise there is at the minute on social media paired with our ever-shortening attention spans. A quick, snappy video that provides a window into your soul will connect and engage your audience more than any other fancy marketing ad or text-heavy website will. It is a much quicker way to build up that 'know, like, and trust' factor.

Whichever medium you use, I highly recommend creating lots of content in advance so you aren't scrabbling around each week for something to talk about. A cohesive theme of content works well across social media, and in blogs and podcasts, as it is not only easier to plan the content around it, but the value is usually greater when subjects are explored over a longer period of time rather than sporadically touched upon. This also helps build consistency and reliability in the relationship with your potential customers. Committing to showing up consistently is incredibly important.

Finally, whether you pick just a couple or a handful of mediums depends on your time and resources. One platform focused upon and done well will be more effective at delivering results than seven platforms that you are doing a poor job at managing. You do, however, risk losing your platform if it is built on what we call 'borrowed land' (i.e. a medium that you don't own the rights to). This includes all the social media platforms—Facebook, Pinterest, LinkedIn, Instagram. I recommend spreading your eggs across at least three baskets, so you are not solely reliant upon one marketing medium or social media platform. An email list is typically considered one of the most valuable marketing assets you can have, because if you have an email list of potential and past customers, you still have a way to directly reach your ideal client if a platform disappears or becomes obsolete. You can make sure that only your ideal client gets into your email list by using a very targeted lead magnet, specific to them. You can also nurture your relationships with your past customers so that they are likely to continue buying from you. Thus, I recommend you select one social media platform, have your own website, and start an email list to begin with. But really, it's up to you to consider the options, think about where your ideal client is, test them, and commit to advertising in the three areas you think will work the best.

Your Objectives and Tracking Measures

Once you have done your research, committed to your mediums, and you have an idea of your own time and resources, you need to figure out your marketing objectives, targets, and tactics for each medium. Your overall aim of marketing will always be to sell your product or service, but this can be broken down into objectives such as demonstrating that you are the expert in your field, growing your network for future collaboration, or showing the personality behind your brand. You might have different objectives for different mediums and knowing what they are will help guide your plan on what content to use. Targets will be things like how many followers or engagement on Instagram you get per month, the percentage of open rates on your emails, or the number of clicks on your Facebook ads. Your tactics are essentially when you will post on social media, how frequently you upload new content, and how long you will spend engaging with your customers. Having clear objectives, targets, and tactics will make it much easier to analyze which of your marketing mediums are working for you, and which aren't.

To run successful marketing campaigns, you have to figure out which marketing mediums and tactics work best for meeting your marketing objectives. There is a phrase that I remember hearing, but don't know who to attribute it to, that 50% of your marketing will work. You just don't know which 50% it is. The goal is to figure it out. And the best approach to take here is to use the scientific method of testing it, measuring it, then changing one variable, testing it, measuring it…etc. on repeat. There are ways to track the effectiveness of your marketing on certain platforms. For example, there are insights on Instagram and Facebook showing you how many people have seen your posts, have clicked on your posts, have visited your site from that post…etc. You can track open rates and click rates on emails sent to your list, you can install pixels, and you can use Google Analytics and your own website provider's analytics—all of which will give you valuable information on what is working and what is not. If you have absolutely no idea how to track and measure the effectiveness of your marketing, however, you need to take time to learn it or make room in your budget to hire someone to do it for you. You don't want to be wasting money on marketing outlets that absolutely aren't working for you. I wasted hundreds of pounds each year on paying for a directory that stopped bringing me customers after just one year before I realized. Analyze constantly and test what works. Try different wording, styles, and images on your posts, and see how the customers respond. But do it by using the scientific method, and not all at once.

If you are advertising on billboards and the radio, or on television, it is much harder to know where your customers found you. You can for sure ask, as I do when speaking to my customers. "Just out of interest," I say, "how did you discover us?" But often, they say they can't remember. They looked at so many, or saw us on some site somewhere, but they were not sure if they could remember which one it was. Not ideal I know. So do your best to measure it, but don't stress if you can't track 100% of where your clients come from. Knowing where the majority come from should help you to figure out where it is worth spending more of your time or resources and where, perhaps, it isn't. After all, if the money you have allocated isn't bringing you any leads/customers, then you can reassess your strategy.

In summary, take the time to come up with a comprehensive marketing strategy—who you are targeting, where they are, how you will reach them, how often you will review it….etc. It will make sure you are taking this aspect of your business seriously. The good thing is that marketing now is so much easier than ever before. So much quicker and so much cheaper. You can literally get into everyone's inbox and line of sight for free, or in exchange for the smallest piece of valuable content you can offer (your lead magnet). You can find your ideal client online and chat with them without being sleazy, without having to find their phone number and cold calling them. And you can reach right across the globe.

Action Prompts

- Get crystal clear on your product or service, and the results or transformation offered

- Figure out who will benefit the most from that transformation and come up with your niche and your ideal client avatar

- Think about what your USP will be and how your personality/experience can be added to magnify this in your business

- Come up with your elevator pitch, key terms to use in your messaging (including pain points), and results your ideal client would likely search for (based on research conducted)

- Brainstorm ideas for the different marketing content you will need (awareness content, consideration content, content that appeals to your ideal client, would be valuable to your ideal client, and also shows your brand values and personality)

- Decide if you will become the face of your brand, or if you aren't, how else can you emotionally connect with your audience and show your values to build that 'know, like, and trust' factor

- Think about how you want your business to be perceived and decide upon your branding to start (your name, logo, colors, fonts, consistency, as well as your values and personality)

- Come up with some 'hook-story-close' sales pitches and sales copy

- Consider your mindset around selling and either get coached on it or figure out if you need extra training

- Figure out where your ideal client hangs out (guess, research, ask, and then test)

- Come up with your marketing budget and assess the advantages and disadvantages of each of the medium options that came up when you researched where your ideal client would be (what do you have the time, money, and aptitude for?)

- Figure out your objectives, targets, and tactics for each medium

- Learn about SEO and how to understand and track your marketing metrics to assess effectiveness and make a plan for tracking (or see if you can hire someone to do this for you)

- Put all of the above into your marketing strategy and assess, review, and adjust regularly

CHAPTER 3
THE EARLY DAYS OF YOUR BUSINESS

After the initial whirlwind of starting our business, we both put a lot of time and effort into ensuring that we were doing the best job we could with regard to delivering a fantastic customer experience. In testing the market early on with just a single bell tent unit (the minimum viable product number), we asked for feedback from our customers and made any significant changes we needed to early on. As I was onsite doing most things myself, I was able and eager to ask customers in person for feedback. I quickly learned that if I just asked, "Was everything ok?" They would always reply, "Yeah, great thanks." But if I changed my question to, "We are always keen to improve our site, is there anything at all that you would have liked to have had provided that wasn't?" or a variation of this, I could always dig out something that we could then add on for our next customers.

As I had no clue what we were doing, I kept looking around at others serving the same space and at what they were offering, so I was very aware of the trends, how customer desires were changing, and what we needed to do to keep up. We took the opportunity to have a break and do some further market research by staying at a competitor's site. We also camped out in our own campsite to get a feel for what we were offering and troubleshoot any problems or inconveniences we found.

In our attempts to deliver a fantastic experience, we both got involved in every single aspect of the business. My partner designed a simple website on an easy-to-use platform and tweaked the physical structures we had put on site to ensure our guests had a great stay, and I got right into the trenches, doing everything else. From creating copy for our ads, to managing customer enquiries and taking bookings, to doing the changeovers in our bell tents, greeting all our customers, chopping logs, doing the laundry and ironing, and yep, even emptying the composting toilet bucket! Now, don't get me wrong, I did *not* enjoy all of these tasks. Unblocking the 'wee pipe' from the overenthusiastic child with the sawdust for the fifteenth time was never on my list of things I wanted to do when I grew up (we started up with composting toilets). However, getting involved and wearing all the hats in my business meant that I knew what was needing to happen in the business to take a customer from inquiring, to having a great experience camping, to leaving happy at the end of their stay. I knew all the front of house requirements and the back of house processes involved, I had built skills in a variety of areas including the all-important ones of resilience and problem solving, I had learned how to do hard things, I had saved money at the start of our journey, and I had a clear idea of what to delegate first when we did hire help.

Because of the above, we tweaked our product/service several times in those early years, aiming to improve the customer experience every time (e.g. we swapped out lower quality items for higher quality items when we could afford to, we simplified certain procedures on site and we cut out certain steps altogether), and we responded to anything we needed to as quickly as we could. This equated to what you most want in your business—happy customers!

* * *

Looking back at how we approached the early days of our business journey, there are a few things I pulled out that I consider vital both to our initial survival and the continued success of our business, and they all relate to one key thing—**being flexible and responsive in**

business. This is where, if your personality type is more of a 'free-spirit, winging it' type like my own, you will come into your own, while the more 'perfectionist, planning ahead' types might struggle. It is also where you will see the benefits of taking my advice to keep your systems, products, services, and business structure simpler at the start.

Be Flexible with Changing Up Your Product/Service

The first area where being flexible early on will pay in the long-term is regarding your product or service. You will have a good idea of what your product or service should start out as from your initial market research and product/service testing, but you can still gain so much value from being open to receiving feedback from your initial customers. For example, let's say you want to release a hat making course online. Your initial market research will have indicated that there was a demand for it and perhaps what the main sections of it should contain. Your beta course (released to just a few readers) may have highlighted any obvious gaps, eliminated small errors in the text, and confirmed it is of value. However, after running the course several times in the first few months, you might receive feedback from the early users that they struggled with a particular section, or lost motivation part way through. This would then be the perfect opportunity to brainstorm how you could implement an accountability factor or additional support, which would add even more value to the course. Simply asking for feedback is one of the best ways to ensure that your product/service is meeting consumer demand but is so often neglected. Feedback in the early days of your business is even more important than in the latter days because your systems and processes are still simple, any infrastructure in place is basic and changes to the product or service can be made easily made. Thus, altering things in the early days could save you thousands of pounds, the risk of getting a negative reputation or being outcompeted by someone else in your market, and lots of time.

Now, this isn't to say that all feedback should be acted upon. But all feedback should be given due consideration. Especially if the customer you have asked has been gracious enough to take the time to give it. All too often, nowadays, it is nigh on impossible to get feedback, even if you ask. Learn to phrase your feedback request so it makes them feel like they would be helping you, rather than criticizing you, and you will have many more willing participants. You can also try to incentivize it, but you have to be careful that you aren't unintentionally bribing them in the process. The best thing you can do is to reduce the number of obstacles in the customers' way by making the process of giving or leaving it as streamlined (simple, easy, and quick) as possible—maybe have a pre-filled in form ready for them or ask for them to complete it personally (people find it much harder to say no face-to-face and even after they have left your premises/you are out of sight, if they promised in person to do it, their own conscience will probably make them leave it for you). People also generally want to help support small businesses, so you are much more likely to get that ever so critical feedback in the early days than when you have grown big later on.

Another way to ensure you are delivering the best value you can give is to use your own product or service and test it out. It seems like such a simple suggestion, but you would be surprised by how many businesses haven't actually tested the products/services they themselves sell. If it isn't something you would usually enjoy using, then get a family member, friend, or focus group to try it. You cannot and should not be relying solely on just a couple of your customers' feedback to ensure you are on the right track. After all, many customers will buy a mediocre product and maybe not have anything too detrimental to say about it, but the business providing that mediocre product will likely never get repeat customers, they won't be recommended on to others, and they are unlikely to rise to any great heights of success with a product that isn't considered to be of exceptional value.

Using the product or service yourself is also likely to help you understand what your customers' feedback means and help you understand how you can serve them better. It's a very different experience to just reading suggestions on a piece of paper, as it you will be personally experiencing the problem in real life.

Another key point to consider here is the overall customer experience. As the saying goes, "the customer knows best". Unfortunately, even where this isn't true, you do want to be aiming to deliver the best experience you can afford to give. Sometimes this isn't possible—an honest mistake may mean that the customer experiences a substandard level of customer service with the product or service in question. In these cases, I have found it is always best to apologize early and ask for forgiveness. Customers end up usually much more amenable if they feel like they are being understood. Even if they are wrong. This is where, I really would advise, that if you do not enjoy dealing with the general public (and their many quirks), you pick a business that serves other businesses. Because you really cannot fake it. If you genuinely don't care, your customers will know it. And faking it is both exhausting and unpleasant for you too. That isn't to say you should allow customers to bully you. You absolutely don't have to do that. Some people are so scared of receiving a bad review, they are effectively being held prisoner by their own customer. You don't have to worry. People can generally always tell when a genuine mistake has been made or when a customer would moan about the sun rising in the east and setting in the west. One bad review won't ruin your business. Your attitude about it will though.

It is also so much easier and cheaper to nurture your existing clients and customers, than to find new ones. So, take the time and energy to build a solid relationship with them. They are then more likely to either give you referrals and recommendations, or come back again and again. Having an actual defined plan in place for encouraging referrals, repeats, and recommendations is also worth making, rather than relying on hope alone (e.g. offering a discount, referral gift). A useful insight here to note is that people generally don't sue relationships—there is lots of guidance for doctors in the United States that recommends they spend longer than 8 minutes in a session with a patient, due to research showing that patients were 90% less likely to sue if something went wrong. This is simply because they felt they had a relationship with that doctor. If you take the time to build a relationship with your clients, benefits will be reaped on both sides.

Be Agile and Responsive to Market Changes

Being agile and responsive to market changes in the early days of your business journey will also be hugely important to your survival and success. This basically means keeping your eyes open and looking around at the market and at others serving the same market as you for changes in consumer desires, buying behavior, trends, and new competition. The benefit of being a new entrepreneur and getting your product/service out there before you have all the 'proper' systems and lengthy protocols set in place, and before you have solidified all of your messaging across all advertising platforms, is that you can easily pivot, or tweak your product/service to either fulfill the evolving need/desire of your customer, or stand out from the rest. If there is a way to figure out the processes and all the steps necessary for creating and delivering your product, then scaling it back to the minimal smallest viable steps and product to keep your business simple, then things can be easily changed with minimal cost if they need to be. The ramifications of any significant changes early on will be small, as you will have fewer third parties involved right at the start, you will have invested way less in the systems, and you may not have any systems in place for some things yet.

This is one of the key advantages you will have over the larger, more well-established, long-standing competition. Embrace the opportunity fully. Do your market research frequently and tweak as needed. If a new competitor comes on the scene with a much-improved product or service and is competing on price with you, you know you need to up your game swiftly—an inferior product or service will not make your business a success.

Outsourcing vs DIY

A lot of new entrepreneurs struggle with knowing what they should outsource right from the beginning and what they should keep in-house. There is no perfect, one-size-fits-all solution for this. It depends entirely on where your talents, skills, and experience lie, how quickly you can learn new tasks, your interests and desire to learn new skills, the urgency with which you want to set up and sell, and the budget you have.

Nonetheless, aside from testing the product yourself and getting involved in dealing with the customers (which I already mentioned should be on your to-do list), there is tremendous value to be obtained from getting involved in all areas of your business at the start, from the process of building the product/service if you can right through to the process of delivering it. By getting involved, you will not only be able to figure out what parts of that business you enjoy and what parts you don't (vital when looking to scale or grow later—see Chapter 5), but it can also help you figure out your own strengths and weaknesses, and what you would consider your unique ability (or zone of genius, as my Leadership coach, Skye Barbour, refers to it as) to actually be.

Getting involved will also help you understand the processes better, which will make you a much more compassionate leader when it comes time to grow your business and have others involved doing those parts for you, as you will be able to explain exactly how you want it done. In getting your own hands dirty, you are more likely to garner respect from your team (that you aren't ever going to ask them to do something that you wouldn't do yourself).

Getting involved will also help you figure out ways you could simplify and streamline processes, save time, cut costs and cut out unnecessary steps, which will pay dividends later. It also means you could draw up checklists, SOPs (Standard Operating Procedures), and quality controls that could be used by third parties when you hire them to ensure the whole process is smoothly followed every time and ensure the product/service is delivered at a consistently high standard.

Having said this, creating your SOPs for each of the necessary tasks in your business is also something I recommend doing any way as early as you can in your new business, even if you have no desire to grow your business beyond yourself. It means that if you ever fall ill, you can ask someone to step in to do the essential tasks, and they will have a clear and easy procedure to follow in order to create the desired result. Sadly, I found this out for myself when I got the flu midway through our busiest season and I had to ask my partner to do all of my tasks—scrambling to write down what needed to be done on bits of paper for him so he didn't forget anything, because I hadn't taken the time to do this in advance. It wasn't that I hadn't thought about it, I had been meaning to sit down and create the systems for months but, as with everything in life, if you don't make it a priority it just keeps getting buried on the to-do list and never gets done. Make sure that you give it enough time and attention, and re-visit it each year as systems evolve and change as the business grows. Even now I am still in the process of streamlining my processes and setting up formal SOPs, (organization and tech are not my strengths, so I hired a coach just to help me get this part right) but every time I work on it, there is a huge sense of relief that comes from knowing everything is organized enough, that someone else could come in and take over from you if needs be.

Another tip worth mentioning here is to develop the habit early in your business to stay ahead if you can with regard to your maintenance tasks (e.g. updating sales and expense records, content creation for marketing, planning scheduled posts…etc.) so that if you do have an unexpected situation come up, you can take a week off using the buffer time you have built in, with things that have already been planned/created, so you don't fall behind and you don't have to outsource (getting the right support in your business to help takes more time than you would think anyhow). Don't leave things until the last minute. Commit to staying up to date and schedule in that time weekly to update spreadsheets, plan content sessions ahead of time, and build in that time buffer for yourself. Trust me – I've fallen behind way too many times, and it is so much harder to keep on track of what is going on in your business (especially with regard to the oh-so-important figures) when you aren't consistently tracking the essentials and making sure you are on top of the day-to-day admin.

Finally, learning the nitty gritty of the individual processes involved in different parts of your business, even if it isn't your expertise, will mean that you are never entirely dependent on another third-party supplier having total control over you and your product—protecting you if they close their business or can't deliver, as you know what is involved and can either step in yourself or delegate effectively to someone else to do what is required. Other incentives are that you will inevitably learn new skills, which will always be useful and potentially transferrable to other projects later; you are teaching yourself the metaskill of doing hard things, even when it doesn't come naturally to you; you will save yourself money early on, so even though it may take a little longer to scale, you won't have the added stress of having to pay others for this work; and finally, when you do scale or sub out the work, you will have learned the process to a point where you can a) advise better on what you need, want, and expect created and b) be able to smell BS a mile off and spot where you may be being ripped off.

Having said all this, if you are 100% sure of your product/service, your values, your product positioning, niche…etc. and your lack of skills/experience in certain areas of your business or your inability to perform a particular vital function in your business is holding you back from actually delivering a great product, or service, then you should absolutely consider outsourcing. I still advocate strongly for DIY whenever possible, but not at the expense of your business. Likewise, if you need certain things in place in your business from the beginning and you simply do not understand them or can't figure it out yourself, consider hiring help (e.g. professional expertise such as legal advisors, accountant, tax advisor). Just make sure when you outsource that you have the budget for it, you seek recommendations first, get quotations in writing, set clear expectations at the start and create clear communication channels to use.

The early days of your business are full of unique challenges and learning opportunities. Do not underestimate the value of being flexible and rolling up your sleeves during this time. Setting yourself up with strong foundations paves the way for a successful future for your business.

Action Prompts

- Decide how you are going to get frequent and vigorous feedback on your product/service (how are you going to ask and how can you remove any obstacles for the customer in order to incentivize them to do it?)

- Figure out if you can objectively test your own product/service, and if not, how you are going to find reliable testers

- Assess your attitude toward your customers and decide on your boundaries ahead of time regarding what is ok and what is not ok regarding how your customers treat you and what your various policies will be regarding customer service

- Schedule time to conduct ongoing market research, track trends, and research the competition (perhaps subscribe to industry newsletters so you stay current)

- Review the steps involved between finding a customer and delivering your product/service to them and see if they could be simplified (could your product/service be simplified further too?)

- Create checklists, SOPs, and quality control processes for each of the delivery process steps

- Build up a bank of work done ahead of time (e.g. plan your content out for your social media a month ahead of time) and schedule in time daily to keep up to date with maintenance tasks (and make it a habit)

- Take a moment to analyze your strengths and weaknesses, what you are willing to do, learn to do, and not do, what your priorities are, and what you can afford to outsource

- Put together a list of tasks to outsource and ask for recommendations

- Write out exact requirements and expectations for what you are outsourcing, a plan for communication, and write down your budget

CHAPTER 4
INVESTING IN YOURSELF

For some bizarre reason, despite my love for learning and having undertaken several courses to help with previous pursuits, as soon as I set up the campsite, I decided to figure it out for myself. All of it. Looking back, I have no idea why I had thought that I should be able to figure it all out or that I should know it already. It was my first 'proper' business. How could I have possibly known everything that I needed to know? I had never learned it. Sure, I had studied business at school, I had transferrable skills from my project management experience, and I had some customer relations skills from my waitressing and bar work. I also had some soft skills like being able to listen and be tactful in my communication that I must have developed from other projects. And I had my personal characteristics, like being diligent, thorough, hard-working…etc. But what I couldn't see in those early days was that there are so many other skills involved in running a successful business and so much knowledge required in order to get certain parts of the business running well.

I think I thought, deep down, that because other people's business success always fascinated me and I always wanted to be an entrepreneur, and because I had dabbled with business in the past, that I would be inherently good at it. I think I also thought that seeking help meant I was cheating on some level, that the truly successful entrepreneurs figure it out for themselves—another classic case of imposter syndrome rearing its ugly head (I go into this in more detail in the mindset chapter). I realize now how dumb this belief was and how it was holding back my progress. It would be like telling a young child that you teaching them how to read and write would be cheating, and expecting them to learn those fundamental skills on their own with no help. We all need to be taught, we all need help sometimes. Don't let mental blocks like imposter syndrome get in the way of your success.

Because of my limiting beliefs, I worked hard but not smart. I tried different things to give different results, but completely on a spontaneous and unscientific trial and error basis. As a result, learning and business growth was much slower and more frustrating than it needed to be in the first few years. Now, no course would have covered exactly everything I needed to know—and many academic courses, sadly, are mostly theory rich with zero practical application. But there were so many ways I could have sped up the process of figuring things out, had I actually decided that it would be helpful to commit to investing in my ongoing learning.

* * *

One lesson that I wish I had learned earlier in my business was to invest in myself. It would have saved me a lot of time, struggles, frustration, and self-doubt. Jim Rohn said it best, "Your level of success will seldom exceed your level of personal development. Learn to work harder on yourself than you do on your job." **Remember that you are the most valuable asset in your business.** (As Skye puts it, "You are the golden goose.") Without you, your business wouldn't even exist. Yet we so quickly forget this as we try to hustle our way to success, also forgetting that if we put value into our brains, even more value will come out. Investing in yourself is ultimately an investment in your business.

Learning the Business Fundamentals

Now, I'm not saying you need to go out and spend a fortune on an MBA, or even a lesser fortune on a marketing course. There is so much information out there for free and with a little digging and due diligence on the source, you effectively have a wealth of knowledge to tap into. If you commit to constant improvement and learning of yourself and your skills just using these initially, it will make your life both inside and outside of your business so much easier.

So, what business fundamentals should you find courses/information/knowledge on first, if you are just setting out in your business journey? I define the business fundamentals and their associated required skills as follows:

- **Product/Service Creation:** Whichever product or service you go for, you need to be good at delivering an excellent experience with it. So, make sure that you acquire whatever skills you need to deliver this product or service, or you risk damaging your reputation before you've even begun.

- **Marketing:** As previously mentioned, not only do you need to do your work regarding figuring out your niche, your messaging, and which platforms to use, you need to learn how to use those marketing platforms to your advantage. There are tons of marketing specialists, social media experts...etc. with great resources to help you master these platforms and understand the tracking metrics within them. You also need to learn how to create good content (whether it be video, blogs, written copy, or photographs) on those platforms that will be engaging to your customer, as you will be the one putting this out there initially.

- **Sales:** If you are not comfortable asking for the sale, particularly if your business will be set up in a way where you are making offers over the phone or in person, getting help with confidence, handling objections, and knowing what to say will be essential.

- **Finance:** Knowing how to handle the money in your business and understanding the accounting and tax basics are crucial skills to develop for running a business well. Even if you outsource accounting early in your business, you still need to understand how to track your finances, what money to be putting aside for tax and paying salaries (including yourself), how to manage cash flow, and how to calculate whether or not particular opportunities are worth pursuing (i.e. what the return on investment will be), in order to make informed decisions about the day-to-day running of your business. Top tip here – set up a separate business bank account from day 1 (I didn't and the resulting headaches of sorting through my finances were hideous and totally not worth it).

- **Organization:** Organization and productivity go hand in hand. Even if you are productive in the moment, poor organization skills will cost you time (and therefore money) later. Thus, if you are not a naturally organized person, I recommend taking courses on basic organization or having someone organized help you at the start. This will help you set up systems in your business, keep everything orderly, and prevent things from falling through the cracks. If you take the time at the start of your business to get organized regarding how certain tasks will be organized, filed, noted, allocated…etc., then you will be winning as your business gets busy later on. This is also where you should consider whether or not certain technology solutions would better serve you than manual ones. If you are not clued up on the tech side, add this to your list to learn the basics on. At a minimum, you will need to do simple things like edit your website, use social media, understand how to track marketing metrics, use a digital calendar...etc.

- **Leadership:** If you have plans to grow your business past yourself, or if you know you will need to hire in help right from the beginning, learning skills in effective delegation, leadership, and communication will be imperative to get the best from your team, so I recommend doing some training in this before you begin.

- **Legal:** Taking a free course will, in no way, be a worthy substitute for getting proper, tailored legal advice for your particular business or circumstance. However, I recommend that you at least understand the basics you need in place before you start trading, so you are protected if a mistake does happen and you know what your legal obligations are regarding your customer. Pay particular attention to customer rights legislation and contracts. If you aren't 100% clear on any part of it, seek legal help to inform you. This will save you time and money later on for sure. This also applies to if you plan to hire help. Get familiar with the legal requirements and processes for hiring, insurance, and accounting if you plan to grow past yourself. You will save yourself so many headaches and potential lawsuits if you get it right at the beginning of your expansion.

- **Customer Service:** This comes naturally to some and not so much to others, so maybe review whether this would apply to you. If you treat the customer how you would like to be treated yourself, you can't go too far wrong, but the better experience you give the customer, the more loyal a customer they are likely to become. In the world of business, a loyal customer that comes back to buy from you time and time again will cost you far less than having to find new ones, they will be more likely to give you a referral/recommendation. So, if you think you need to brush up on your people skills, do it now.

Once you are confident that you have the fundamental business skills and knowledge nailed, make sure that once you kick off on your business journey, you don't forget to keep learning. Obviously there will be a huge amount of learning on the job, but it is easy to get swept up in the day-to-day running of your business and forget that there will be a ceiling as to how far you can go before you reach the limit of your skillset and knowledge and need to learn more.

In our normal nine-to-five jobs, it is commonplace to find ourselves automatically enrolled on the latest CPD (Continuing Professional Development) course as a requirement by the boss. Your CPD in your business should be no different. Or rather, I'd say, it is even more important than when you are working for your employer, as you can leverage your learning into much greater levels of success in your business than you can for theirs. Thus, commit early on to a timeframe and plan for learning, and stick to it. My top tip would be to make a plan at the beginning of each year with what areas you would like to be improving within each quarter, and then look for particular courses you could undertake and schedule them in advance, so they actually get done. Along the way, however, I highly recommend researching some good business podcasts that you can listen to regularly, while you are driving, doing housework, or walking the dog. You will be amazed by how much valuable yet free content there is available and by how much you can absorb just by immersing yourself in it while your brain is in idle mode. It will also open your eyes to expanding your network somewhat by figuring out whose work you like and who may be good to connect with in the future, either as a customer or as a collaborator if it fits with your business.

Hiring a Business Coach/Consultant

An alternative to the usual DIY courses would be to consider hiring a business coach at each stage in your business and planning this into your budget and timeline in advance. Perhaps at the end of each quarter, you look to hire a business coach that specializes in a different area of expertise to review your progress and discuss and formulate strategies for where you could improve. Simply discussing your business with someone objective, outside of it, and then seeing your business from that perspective can be so eye-opening. Often you will see new opportunities in front of you that you wouldn't have been able to see before and this alone may pay for the cost of it. Business coaches can also help by holding you accountable. We are often much more likely to do what we say we are going to do if we have someone external to report to about it. Also, if you book your session in advance, you are likely to be much more motivated to have something worth showing them, which will help get you over the initial reluctance to putting yourself out there.

The entrepreneur's journey can be a lonely one. Often, you may find yourself as the only entrepreneur in a room, and your friends and family may be mostly employees, so you will have no one to share your ups and downs with who can empathize with you through common experience. Finding a business coach you can relate to and enjoy working with will make the experience of working to achieve your business goals much more fun. Reach out to those coaches who inspire you and listen to their advice. Also, your business coach will likely have a fantastic network of other entrepreneurs in similar stages as you in their business and some great contacts that you would benefit from connecting with for educational purposes, collaboration purposes, and support. You can never have too many business friends.

Hire a Life/Mindset Coach

On top of hiring a business coach to help you to look at your figures, marketing, and strategy, and guide you to try new things, I highly recommend that you also book some 1:1 sessions with a life/mindset coach around the same time. If you have no idea what I am talking about, please let me explain.

Often, we try to just hustle our way through the activity that we think we should be doing, which sometimes can work for a short period of time, but more often than not we struggle to get motivated to do the thing consistently, or we become totally demotivated by the fact that we aren't seeing results, so we quit. We frequently find ourselves self-sabotaging our journey onto success, perhaps by setting up a schedule for ourselves or a plan that we know will likely get us to our goal and then not following it. We procrastinate by checking our emails and notifications on Facebook, or by doing other household tasks, and telling ourselves that they are urgent and need to be addressed now. Sometimes, our nemesis is people pleasing and not being able to say no to distractions caused by others, in case they think badly of us. Sometimes, we want to do so much at once, or take on so much in our business and home life combined that we find ourselves overwhelmed and not doing any of it well. Perhaps we have a deep-seated fear of putting ourselves out there online, and that people may 'find out' that we don't know as much as them (the old imposter syndrome kicking in again), or we have a fear of going all in on our businesses and then failing, and having to face the shame of it.

Stepping up as an entrepreneur means you will inevitably find yourself on a rollercoaster of emotions. And it is completely normal. But all of the above are mindset issues. And while fighting through on your own is possible, chances are you are limiting your own potential without even realizing and you are also creating an unpleasant experience along the way, which you really don't have to do. The amazing thing is that your mindset issues can be solved.

I truly believe that investing in continual mindset work is one of the most important investments you can make, not just for your business, but for your physical health, mental health, your relationships and your happiness. This is why I've written a whole chapter on mindset, which is the last chapter of this book, and why I fell into the life coaching world in the first place.

Document Your Personal Growth

One thing I also wish I had done was document my personal entrepreneurship journey from the start. Journaling and photographs are a great way to document your journey throughout your business without it taking up too much time, and they are so lovely to look back upon, to see how far you have come. And the same goes for what courses you took, what you learned, and the mental challenges you faced and overcame. It is easy to forget how much we have grown and stay focused on how far we still have to go, but on those days where you feel disheartened by how much you have still yet to learn, a simple glance back through your journal or photobook will give you a sense of accomplishment and the motivation to carry on.

Action Prompts

- Commit to yourself right now that you are willing to constantly invest in your continued personal development

- Conduct a self-audit to assess your strengths and weaknesses in both your skills and knowledge, and compare them against the skills and knowledge that are considered as business fundamentals

- Decide where you lack knowledge and skills and search for reputable sources for learning this information

- Plan out the next few quarters and what other courses you will look to continue with

- Research a handful of good business and marketing podcasts and start listening

- Budget for and schedule a call with a business and mindset coach either quarterly or every 6 months to see what areas you need to work on to move your business forward, and if they have any programs you would benefit from working through

- Think about your end vision for growing or scaling your business and put in a provisional date for when you might need to look into taking on more staff. Allocate time prior to this to brush up on the latest regulations, legal requirements, and skill building for hiring a team and delegating

- Think about how you will document your journey easily and in an organized manner. This includes what you learn (so it is easily accessible to access when needed), what challenges you faced (and how you felt during and after), and your progress (real metrics of the number of clients, money made, assets acquired, and milestones reached)

CHAPTER 5
CREATING A BUSINESS NOT A JOB

I'm quite an enthusiastic person by nature. I get easily excited by shiny new things and, as I am also rather ambitious (and impatient), I react the same way with opportunities. Needless to say, when I had filled all three bell tents with customers in that first summer, I got overexcited by the fact that there was a market for what we were selling, that the customers seemed really pleased with the overall experience they were having from us, and that I had more demand than I could meet. And the next year, I did what I considered to be the natural thing to do—I bought more tents, more bedding, created new pitches and set them up, and then updated the campsite directories we were on. My partner built more showers and toilets, as well as a hand-crafted, wood-fired hot tub. I didn't take the time to stop and think about what growing would mean in terms of the jobs that needed to be done during the busy periods or the storage needed both during and at the end of the season. I had created more than double the amount of work to be done, but it was still just me doing it.

So, at that time, I had seven bell tents set up, which each took around an hour to clean and two hours to wash, dry, and iron the linen for each one. There were also several toilet and shower facilities, two kitchen areas, a hot tub, firepits, bins, and a handful of camping pitches that I was managing, cleaning, and preparing for the next set of guests. I was still handling and answering all phone call and email enquiries, taking bookings manually, processing the return of deposits manually, and greeting every single camper when they arrived to welcome them and give them a tour of the site.

What I found, was that even when our site wasn't fully booked, there was so much still to do that I was working from 7:00 am until midnight, seven days a week with maybe just an hour off each evening for dinner. I was skipping lunch altogether most days and eating breakfast on the run. Our house had also turned into a laundromat/sundries warehouse. This was pretty much how it was, from opening in April until closing in October. Twice during the summer, my partner and I attempted to take the afternoon off, once for a BBQ with friends and once for a birthday party on the beach, and found that by the time we had finished all the jobs on the campsite and got to the destination, the party had finished and people were making their way home.

Needless to say, my partner was cross with me for being too gung-ho and taking on so much, and I was exhausted. At the end of our second summer, I had reached burn out. Not so bad I was hospitalized, fortunately, but sick of the campsite and drained of enthusiasm, inspiration, and joy for it. I had gotten stuck in the mindset that if I did it all myself, I would be saving us money. As I had invested so much so quickly, I desperately wanted to breakeven quickly and thought doing it myself would be the quickest way.

I had effectively created a summer job for myself. Worse still, I wasn't paying myself anything out of the business, so it was actually more like a volunteer summer position that I no longer received any joy or sense of accomplishment from. The day-to-day tasks themselves were boring and monotonous. I had done them all a thousand times before. I was spending so much time working in the business that I had no time to work *on* the business (i.e. focus on adding in new ideas, analyzing our strategy and figures, improving our delivery systems or improving our marketing—even though this was what excited me most about business). I had no time for learning. I had no time for myself or any of my relationships. I even found myself so exhausted at the end of each day that I couldn't find the energy to actually engage in conversation with my customers and build those important relationships, despite the fact that this was another part of the business I actually enjoyed. I felt stale and my brain felt like it was shrinking. Sure, we were making money, we were super busy, and our customers were having a whale of a time. It was still fulfilling our original goal of having a business we could work in during the summer that enabled us to travel during the winter months. But instead of feeling proud, I was so disappointed in myself that instead of creating a thriving business that I loved, I had created a job that I was beginning to resent.

* * *

Although my over-enthusiasm is mostly to blame, there were a multitude of reasons why I created what felt like a job rather than a business. I didn't take the time to create a vision for what I wanted my business to look like ultimately, I forgot to value my own time, I hadn't set in place the systems I needed before growing the business, I wasn't maximizing my own productivity, I had mindset and money blocks stopping me from hiring in help and I hadn't set up boundaries for my own self-care and family time. I now know better (although even now there are areas I am still working on improving and shaping into what I want), so I will share with you what you can do to avoid growing your business reactively and creating a job rather than a business. I'll also share tips on how to grow it intentionally, if that is your ultimate goal.

Creating a Vision

Once you have gotten going in your business and you have found a product/service you enjoy providing, one that is liked by your customers and that you are committed to running as a proper business, I highly recommend that you sit down and create a vision for yourself of what you want your business to look like. You will have done part of this when considering whether or not ultimately the business idea you have could fit into your ideal lifestyle, but like I said with the bakery example, you won't get a full understanding of what a business will involve and what you will like until you actually give it a proper go. After all, too rigid a plan at the start will mean that you are likely to miss potential opportunities in those early days. A rigid plan may stifle new ideas you may want to explore and it can also put a lot of unnecessary pressure on you at the beginning, when really you should be playing with what works, what doesn't, what feels good…etc. However, once you have gotten going, you have a good idea what the business model entails, your customers are happy, and things are working, then you should explore what exactly you want out of the business ultimately, what vision you have for it, and how it will fit into your lives.

When I started, all I wanted was to have my own business. And I got exactly that. But then once I had taken the plunge and was running it, I got so wrapped up with the day-to-day running of it, that I didn't take the time to come up with a long-term vision of what I wanted out of the business. And this lack of long-term vision meant that I inadvertently went off track. I also forgot the other reasons I had wanted to be an entrepreneur in the first place (e.g. time freedom, financial freedom, coming up with new ideas and implementing them). I focused solely on the purpose of my business being to deliver a great experience to customers and make some money in the process so we could travel in the winter. And that was about it. I had no vision for beyond the next year. As a result, we didn't change anything up. We tweaked a few things to make the customer experience better each year, but I didn't give any time to picturing what I wanted to the business to become or even how much I wanted to earn from the business, and I didn't bother setting any goals or targets on sales or revenue that would make me work smarter to help take me there. I just planned on working hard each year to make a bit more money each time. I hadn't given any thought to the fact that if I doubled the amount of pitches and thus, customers, I was also doubling the work for myself, which wouldn't be sustainable if I wanted the business to grow bigger again. I had fallen foul to incremental thinking, rather than big thinking.

If I could do it over again, I would have taken the time to figure out what I wanted from the business, where I wanted to take it and how I wanted my life to fit into it. From that overarching vision, it would then have been possible to make a rough framework to guide each of the next few years, and from there create targets for sales and profits that would have focused our attention. This would have still given us the flexibility to vary things and change direction if we saw fit, but it would have provided a framework under which we could make decisions in a less reactive way, while considering the overall purpose of the business and its role within our lives. Once you are in business, it will be easy for you to spot other business opportunities and you will find other people will have strong opinions on what you should do with yours—so having this framework can also be a very helpful reminder to assess whether or not those opportunities and suggested directions are in your best interest.

Having targets for sales, marketing, and profit each year is also a great tool to use both for motivation purposes and to ensure that you are celebrating your successes along your business journey. Having both end goals and strategic goals for each of these will help you keep your eye on the money and the figures (an important side note here—don't make revenue the sole goal at the expense of profit, as the saying goes, "revenue is a vanity game, profit is where the sanity is"). Constantly reviewing progress and analyzing what is and isn't working is imperative to creating a successful business. Without knowing, tracking, and reviewing your marketing, sales, profits, expenses…etc. on a regular basis, you will essentially just be spinning your wheels like we did.

It may be that when you start your business, your end goal is to sell it off for profit, rather than keep it as your own. This is so helpful to know as you grow, so that your focus is on creating a sustainable business that someone else would take on, rather than you being reactive to every opportunity and creating a business that is either so bespoke that you couldn't sell it on to someone else or so random in what it offers that no one else would actually want it. Just having this as a goal will mean that you will be keeping a closer eye on how much you need to be turning over and what your margins need to look like in order to be considered as a worthwhile investment for a buyer, so it will effectively give you your annual goals to be motivated by.

Another reason having some clarity over your vision for your future business is useful is that you can then make clear decisions early on as to how and when you grow or scale your business. Typically, new entrepreneurs are super impatient to get to some arbitrary level that they think equates to 'successful', so they grow their business prematurely without due care and forethought. Having a clear plan in place as to when you think you would like to grow (it can be based on revenue, rather than timings) will prevent you from being reactive to every opportunity, jumping the gun, and making impulsive decisions before you have considered the plan and before you have prepared yourself to make the necessary changes.

The last reason to have a vision for how you want your business to look at the end is that you want to ensure you are consciously building a business that supports the lifestyle you want, not just ultimately, but in the whole journey of building it. To have a sustainable, enjoyable business, you need to plan it into and around all the other aspects of your life. You can make allowance for the early stages to be a bit more busy as you find your feet and set up the initial parts, but it is very important not to accept the notion that having a business means that your family life, relationships, and physical and mental health go on the back-burner indefinitely. It simply will not be a sustainably successful business if you do not set it up to be that way, while giving yourself enough time to rejuvenate and enjoy the rest of the things you do in your life. You will just burn out. Or you will make a success of it, but then have no one around you to share your success with. So figure out what kind of lifestyle you want and how your business could fit into it, and then get clear on a vision that will enable you to attain success in your business, while also fitting in the lifestyle you want. Once you have it clear in your mind as a vision, then you can put systems in place to ensure it becomes reality (I'll expand on this later).

It was only when we had closed for the winter, at the end of that second season, that I regained the headspace to realize that I was not running the business the way I wanted to and to understand the benefits of having a vision. Just taking the time to think over what I didn't like about how I was running it created the space for me to think about how I wanted to be running it, and from this I envisioned the possibility **I could ultimately shape the business to be what I wanted it to be.**

Valuing Your Own Time

It's easy to forget when no one is paying you, or when you are working on the back of house tasks in your business, that your time is valuable.

You need to recognize that at a certain point in your business, your time, as the business creator and thinker who is able to create more value, revenue, and profit within your business, is worth more than the money you will be paying out for someone else to do the tasks that don't generate more value within the business. This is not because those tasks aren't important, but because in outsourcing them, it will free up your time so that you can spend more time working *on* the business (and *on* creating more value) rather than *in* the business. Afterall, who else will come up with the business strategy, the marketing strategy, and be the key decision maker in your business? No one. That's your job. And in remembering to value your time, you will focus on the tasks that generally will take your business to new heights, rather than just spinning your wheels. Work out what your time is worth to the business (i.e. what an hour of your time could make in your business) and pay yourself a salary. This way, when your business is busy and you are generating profit, but you find yourself working 15 hour days to get through work that could be outsourced to someone on a lower hourly rate than you, you will see the value in outsourcing and then you can focus on your zone of genius in the business, instead of being tempted to do it yourself, under the erroneous mindset of 'it's cheaper and easier'.

If the only way you are staying afloat financially in your business is if you are doing it all yourself (for little to no money), then something has to change. You need to create more value for your customers or find more customers in order to benefit from economies of scale in your expenses. **Your business won't ever become viable if you are just discounting your own worth to keep it afloat,** and if you aren't paying yourself a salary or making any profit, you will find it extraordinarily difficult to stay motivated and do the high-quality work you need to be doing for your business to survive. I highly recommend researching the concept of 'Profit First' (written about by Mike Michalowicz) to ensure that you are focusing on creating profit in your business first and valuing your time. However, once you are outsourcing to someone else, make sure you really do use the time freed up effectively to create more value in your business (I'll share ways to improve your productivity later). Don't waste it.

Systems and Finances

As you can imagine, I now strongly advocate against growing your business before you are ready, before you have the money to, and before you have the systems in place that will allow you to grow without you needing to treble your hours and work yourself into the ground. If your business model requires you to start with a team at the beginning in order to turnover enough to cover your running costs, then make sure you have sufficient systems for each step in your product or service delivery, working capital (a buffer of cash), clear communication channels, and a clear management strategy in place. And then stay at this size until you have maxed out your capacity for delivering at that and have the systems in place to expand further.

Another key point to make here, regarding having a buffer of cash, is that as soon as you can, I recommend putting away a portion of your profits toward an emergency fund (separate from your day-to-day working capital for cash flow) and potentially toward insurance, just in case your business experiences a significant downturn in revenue, as a result of something out of your control (e.g. a global pandemic—I wrote this during our Government enforced lockdown due to COVID-19—or even if you fall ill and can't work for a while). It could easily be the difference between whether or not you have a business to return back to when things resume as usual.

But you have to have clear guidelines as to when you use it, or you will find yourself dipping into it for every latest gadget and machine instead of working smarter to increase your revenue and decrease your costs.

Productivity Tools

Making sure that you are using what time you do have effectively and efficiently in your business is a must before you consider growing. That way, you know that when you do outsource tasks, hire in help, or pay for automation, you know the time saved isn't being wasted. Batch tasking was a total game changer for me. This is where you focus on the same type of work for a concentrated period, rather than switching between tasks. I used to create a single marketing post a day for each social media platform, coming up with the idea on the fly, and posting it every evening. I found that some evenings were more challenging than others if I was tired and I didn't stick with the overall strategy regarding what my content was about. This usually meant that I would post something that was a little bit irrelevant to what my business was about or what my ideal client wanted to hear. Worse, it would take me ages to find a single photo, come up with a single caption, upload it, find the hashtags…etc. It was, for sure, a total waste of time. Batching the social media work for a month or longer at a time, meant I could come up with a general theme, find 30 photos I could use, batch-write all the content in one, search for and list them all, and schedule them in advance, which totaled a fraction of the time that the everyday shenanigans would take me.

Time theming is another productivity tool I highly recommend (i.e. theming your days regarding what your focus will be for the day) that helps ensure that you are batching, that certain things within your business are getting their due time and attention and not being neglected, and that you are allocating time to work both in your business and *on* your business regularly. For example, Fridays could become 'Financial Fridays'—where you make sure that your expense tracking sheets are up to date, invoices are sent out, payments are chased, and figures are analyzed and measured against your targets and strategy. Mondays could be 'Marketing Mondays'—where all social media posts are batched and scheduled, copywriting for your website and other marketing materials are done…etc.

Time blocking, where you block out sections of your day to focus on certain tasks, is a similar trick you can use to address each area of your business in a focused block of time, as it aims to eliminate distractions, reduce task-switching, and improve focus for that set period of time. A method of time blocking that I use is called the "Pomodoro Technique", where I work for a focused 25 minutes on a single task, take a 5-minute break, and then repeat.

Breaking your yearly goals down into quarterly objectives and then breaking them into smaller mini-goals or tasks is incredibly useful. I find this not only helps to improve focus but also helps ensure that you are spending time within your business on a weekly basis (i.e. you are working on tasks that ultimately help bring in revenue, create sales, or grow your business, rather than spending too much time on the urgent, but non-important, day-to-day firefighting tasks). Take your overall quarterly strategy objectives that you have taken from your overall vision and your annual goal and at the beginning of each month, break down what three key tasks you want to be focused on during that month, which will help move your business toward those goals. Then at the start of each week, figure out the three main tasks that will help move your business forward, and then pick three daily tasks that works toward achieving these weekly goals. Plan these the night before and tell someone, if you can, what your plan is (this will help make you more accountable to achieving them). Aim to focus on working on your daily three first, before you get to all the daily firefighting and running of your business, and you will amaze yourself with how far you will come.

Another productivity tip I recommend doing is to work on building some good business habits early in your business. Habits are helpful for ensuring that you are consistent in your business. Once they are engrained, they require little mental effort or motivation for them to just be part of your behavior. This will serve you so well in your business. For example, depending upon your business, it may benefit you to incorporate a networking habit once a week where you commit to spending 30 minutes a week online, connecting with and building relationships with other business owners or potential customers. Note that this is not in a sleazy, creepy, cold calling type way, but in a genuine 'I want to get out and expand my network, provide value where I can, let people know what I do, meet interesting people and build relationships' way. You will find at the end of the year, after having done this consistently every single week, that you will have expanded your network massively, yet with minimal effort. Another good habit to build is a 'weekly bank reconciliation' habit or a 'look at my goals every morning' habit. The easiest way to habit formation is to start with a mini-habit (just doing the first two minutes of the habit) and consistently repeat it day after day, preferably at the same time of the day, and associated with something else that you already do every single day. **In the long run, good business habits will serve you better than almost anything else.** They will help reduce stress and help keep you organized.

The last thing I will mention here is that I find that at the end of each week, taking the time to look back over what I did and didn't achieve, where I stuck to my schedule and where I didn't and why, what I learned during the week, and plan for the next week based on what I learned, massively impacts how productive I am the following week. On weeks where I don't do this, I go off track and never get as much done, nor do I feel as good about what I do get done. Have a go and see if it works for you.

Self-Care, Boundaries, and Your Non-Negotiables

Right at the beginning of your business, it will be hard to not work into your evenings and weekends, particularly if you are starting it up while still working full time (as many people do). The initial stages of a business are also usually more hectic because of the sheer number of tasks you will be undertaking at the beginning yourself, your reluctance to delegate or automate until you know it is working and you have money coming in, the newness of tasks meaning they take more time, and your own lack of skills, knowledge, and inefficiencies. Systems take time to be refined and made more efficient, which is something you will only figure out by having a go and seeing where they can be made more so.

The temptation will be to work twice the number of hours early on and give up all free time, health time, and sleep. Now, you may have to cut down on certain activities and you may need to stop doing other things altogether, but you should still be making sure you are not compromising on the things you need and value most in life. **There is no excuse for starting a business and putting yourself at risk of both relationship and health failure.** It is just not worth it.

Design your business around your life and the lifestyle you want from the start (not just when you want to grow), or you may find that in pushing through the stress and struggle in the early years, you sabotage the relationships with the people that were the whole reason you wanted to make the business work in the first place.

You need to take a long hard look at the business you are looking to do, your budget, your timeframe, and your expectations to see if you can limit the amount hours you work on it so that you can find some balance in your life (e.g. a work-life balance, social interactions, relationships, hobbies, rest, sleep, and exercise). These aspects of life so often and so easily get neglected when we start our businesses in the pursuit of success, but having a well-rounded life as you grow your business will supercharge your energy, creativity, problem solving skills, and your attitude and positivity that you bring to the business. I know this sounds challenging. But it may be worth reconsidering your expectations as to how quickly you want the business to take off. I agree with Bill Gates here when he said, "Most people overestimate what they can do in one year and underestimate what they can do in ten years." Often, we are putting too much pressure on ourselves to deliver what are already unrealistic expectations. Instead, be in it for the long game.

What I recommend, instead of putting so much pressure on yourself to get a certain number of sales in early, is having a slightly bigger buffer of money at the start and moving your expectation timelines to further out so you aren't compromising your health and your relationships in an attempt to breakeven that little bit sooner.

I also recommend making key decisions about your work/play boundaries in advance—what you are prepared to give up, cut back on, and what and who your key priorities are in your life. Be disciplined in sticking to those decisions and boundaries. If you do this, you will more than likely find that the work you churn out in your working hours will be so much more productive and valuable than it would have been if you were working double the hours and were run-down, both emotionally and physically. You will also be much more focused and more likely to do the work in the time allocated.

Once your business is set up and you find that you are productive, focusing, and working effectively and efficiently, if the number of tasks you need to be getting done each day is still exceeding the hours you have available, then you need to look at either automating more or delegating and the cost vs. benefit of that to you and your business.

One thing I found helpful, once I realized that I had lost all balance in my life and that something needed to change, was taking time to figure out my 'non-negotiables'. This was what I wanted to incorporate daily or weekly that would mean I got sufficient rest and rejuvenation time, and that meant I was honoring what I valued. For example, I committed to take two 20-minute walks outside with my dog daily, have dinner with my parents once a week, prioritize getting eight hours sleep…etc. And then I worked on building them into my life as lifestyle habits (same methodology as for the business habits). If you do this, then you know that no matter how hard you are working, you are still fitting in the most important things for you, your health, and your loved ones. And that these will get done, no matter what.

A good tip to remember when you are feeling pushed and pulled by the needs of your business and start to give in to the temptation to work on or quit on your non-negotiables, is to remember your deep 'why'. This should help you figure out if what you are about to spend time on is worth it or not. Because you have to remember, **the business is not your life.** It's just a business. It's one part of your life. And that's something important to never lose sight of.

Growing Your Business

When growing your business, assuming you know there is sufficient marketplace demand, the first step to take is to list all the tasks you currently do in your business to survive and deliver your product or service, and consider what the impact of growing your business would have on this list. Are there additional tasks that would come as a result of growing the business? Would the tasks stay the same, but increase in number? Or would they stay the same, but you would end up benefiting from economies of scale by growing? Consider how many hours you are currently working within the business and *on* the business, and whether or not this extra work will be too much for you to handle on your own.

The next step is to consider each task you currently do and each additional task that will come from growing, as to whether or not it falls within your 'talent zone' (as Skye calls it—i.e. are you good at it, or enthusiastic to improve upon it, or do you enjoy doing it?). Also factor in which are the tasks you do that are uniquely you. These are the tasks you do that actually add your personality into the business (e.g. perhaps you do some front of house tasks that actually help sell your brand or add value to your business regarding the customer's experience). These tasks are ones you want to ensure you keep and make sure you have time for.

The next step is to consider the list of tasks and whether or not each task fits into your ideal lifestyle vision of how you want your business to run. Are these tasks you ultimately want to keep doing yourself?

Finally, consider at this point whether or not you could hire someone else to do that particular task for you, at a cost that would be worth freeing up your time to then go focus on creating more value in your business elsewhere. Creating SOPs for each additional task (i.e. the exact steps involved in each task) will then help identify the exact amount of time each of the tasks take and therefore how much time you could save in your business if you were to either automate these tasks or delegate these tasks to someone else. From this list, you will be able to work out what tasks you want to take off your list for automation or for delegating to someone else, to manage growing in a sustainable and profitable way.

Automating Tasks

With regard to automating certain tasks, it is absolutely worth considering early in your business (once your business is ticking along but even before you think about growing) whether or not the time savings of automating would be worth the cost—i.e. would it mean you could focus your time on other higher-level tasks that would ultimately generate more profit in your business and thus give you a better return on your investment, rather than you spending time doing this yourself? Nonetheless, when you think about growing your business, it is absolutely something to consider. We are super lucky in the age that we now live, that technology to automate administrative tasks and speed up the process is so easily accessible and affordable to us now, that it would be foolish not to do so for certain tasks. This is something I wish I had looked into several years earlier in our business, as administrative tasks (answering emails, sending out directions, manually updating spreadsheets) took up a huge amount of my time and meant that I couldn't be spending that time improving my marketing or meeting my customers to make sure they were having an excellent time (all things that would have given me a better return in the future). The alternative to hiring the tech to automate this could be to hire an assistant (virtual or otherwise) who is specifically skilled at a particular task. This means you are only paying out for the one task and not having to create extra work for your assistant just to keep them busy, which is what you would end up doing if your first step was to hire an employee in-house. Same as with the tech though, take the time to weigh up the value vs. cost in delegating vs. doing the work yourself. You don't want to be taking on staff at all until you know your time is more valuable within the business doing other tasks than the task at hand. However, as I have mentioned already, if the task at hand requires a higher level of skill than you have, then you need to be hiring in help for that task as in doing so you will be ultimately creating for value for the business overall.

Another thing to consider when automating and when considering technology within your business is that you should either learn the tech yourself or commit to paying someone else to get the tech right for you (both early on and on an ongoing basis). In our society, people are getting more and more impatient for instantaneous answers, communication, and gratification. For example, there are tons of studies that show that a slow loading website actually will cost you sales, as it will be the first barrier that you have to get people through in the conversion process. Glitchy websites or problems with the payment systems you have, are also no good for the bottom line. You want to spend money to ensure that you are removing as many barriers as you can so that your customers find you easily and can buy from you easily. So much marketing involves technology nowadays too, so you want to iron out any kinks early on. They will only cost you more in the long run if you don't, particularly when you have grown in size.

Action Prompts

- Remember your 'why' for setting up a business

- Formulate a vision for the future of your business (even if hazy at this point, you can redo it once your business is up and running and you know the ins-and-outs of it)

- Set a recurring date for when you will reassess your vision, based on what has happened in your business up until that point, and adjust your long-term vision each time

- Break your vision down into a framework with annual marketing, revenue, and profit goals, and then decide upon your quarterly and monthly targets to aim for

- Stick your targets up somewhere you can see them daily, and schedule in time each week to assess your progress and your timeframe and adjust if needed

- Read the book 'Profit First' and decide if it will be beneficial for you to run your business this way. Consider what salary you will be paying yourself to begin with and thus, what your time is worth

- Set up a separate bank account for your emergency fund to be paid into and create rules around using it

- Consider each task involved in your business for it to exist and run successfully. Objectively consider whether the SOPs could be made more efficient, and if it is worth your time to be doing them or if it is worth either automating or delegating them out (i.e. is there a way your time could be adding more value to the business doing tasks other than these?). Are your communication channels and management processes as efficient and effective as they could be?

- Consciously decide at what point in your business you will want to grow it further. This could be based on revenue, profit, no. of customers, no. of hours you are working…etc. Consider whether this time frame might negatively impact the customer's experience, the costs of running the business, or your lifestyle. Is this acceptable to you?

- Take some time to try out some productivity tools and find what works best for you

- Figure out which good business habits you want to incorporate into your daily and weekly life, where they fit in best, and start doing them

- Take a moment to decide on what your non-negotiables and your boundaries will be, and how you will turn these into lifestyle habits that stick

CHAPTER 6
YOUR MINDSET IS EVERYTHING

When I originally set up my business, without realizing it or consciously choosing it, I felt confident in my decision to set it up. I had looked around, done my market research, seen what seemed to work, and felt confident that I could deliver the same standard of service to my customers. With this feeling of confidence driving my actions, I had a business up and running within a week.

As we took more bookings, my confidence grew, and the belief that there was sufficient demand and that we were doing a good job empowered me to reinvest the money we were making straight back into the business, buy more tents, create more facilities, and expand.

I then found that I couldn't physically cope with the increased amount of work I had created for myself, I lost all sense of balance in my life and that's when I started to loathe the work I was doing. My enthusiasm for it all disappeared. Hence, I found it particularly hard to get re-motivated in the winter to work on the business, prepare for the subsequent opening, and try new things. When summer came, I found myself in much the same position. Struggling with trying to fit everything in, juggling home life, family life, back of house tasks, front of house tasks, and everything between. It didn't help that I was still involved in various construction projects and I had set up a partnership with my beloved sister to run some holiday rentals as well. I was spreading myself thin and neglecting all the other important things in life. I was working harder, not smarter, and being reactive rather than proactive, regarding decision-making in all of the businesses and projects I was involved in.

Even though our business was profitable, we were delivering a fantastic service to our customers (we had a 99% positive feedback review rate), and we had built up the business ourselves with minimal help, guidance or instruction along the way, we weren't doing as well as what I would have liked. It wasn't that I didn't know how to improve upon the business either, I knew what our shortcomings were and what needed to be done. Yet, I completely got in my own way. I would decide to grow the business larger again so we could benefit from economies of scale, and then change my mind, thinking I couldn't possibly fit more in. I tried outsourcing and then found I was still doing a lot of the work myself, so the next time I would say I was going to outsource, I would then back-track when I thought of the challenges involved, remind myself that it didn't work last time, and question if it was worth it. I found myself frequently confused, overwhelmed, and doubting that we could ever have a work-life balance and still have a profitable business. I was playing it small. And it was frustrating the hell out of me.

I finally looked outside of myself to figure out if there was a better way and I read up on human behavior, psychology, and mindset. Why we do what we do, why we don't do what we say we will do, and what we actually want to do. This stuff had always interested me—I had studied biology in university and loved the animal behavior, human physiology, and evolution mix that the course involved. I had always been fascinated by the brain and what amazing things humans can do. Combining everything I already knew, with a mix of new knowledge of business, personal development, habit development, and the ingredients of success led into me discovering life (aka mindset) coaching. And my various struggles all started to make sense.

* * *

The pivotal lesson I learned was that having a well-managed mind and an unshakeable mindset is integral to every single part of your business. **Business success isn't overnight and it isn't always easy.** There is no magic pill or one-size-fits-all solution (despite the many get-rich-quick schemes that are promised on social media ads nowadays). It is a constant experiment of tweaking things, trying new things, finding customers, keeping customers, and moving with the times. It is a journey filled with taking risks, putting yourself out there, opening yourself up for criticism, pushing through hard times, making yourself do things you don't like doing, and overcoming various challenges. And if you don't have the skills to manage your mind and master your emotions in that journey, you will inevitably hit a glass ceiling.

Even as I improved upon our systems and marketing and learned more each year of our business (so it was slowly being shaped into something I wanted), I still found that I struggled with certain recurring problems—confusion as to what to do next, overwhelm at the sheer number of tasks I was confronted with daily, not enough time, fear of taking risks regarding hiring or trying radical new things and failing, times where I procrastinated when I knew I should be getting on with a particular task, worrying about money and the competition, and struggling with doubt in myself and the potential in the business. I put it down to me just not doing a good enough job each time. But deep down, I knew I was the one getting in my own way. Investing in life coaching in my fifth year of business was one of the smartest moves I ever made. It gave me so much insight into why I had struggled with the things I had and where, had I just taken the time to sort my mindset out, I could have had a much easier time of it. Nonetheless, I am thankful I went through the experience exactly as I did, or else I wouldn't know what I know now and I wouldn't be able to share my story and the lessons I learned with you.

So, what do I mean when I say mindset? This is your collective thinking and beliefs that affect how you feel, what you do, and ultimately what results you create in your business and life. Your mindset will determine whether or not you quit when times get hard, whether or not you are willing to do what is necessary to succeed, whether you choose instant gratification rather than long-term achievement and whether or not you are able to reach that highest level of success or if you instead, self-sabotage your chances.

Looking back at my business journey, it is now blatantly clear how my mindset had shifted from starting the business as confident, enthusiastic, and positive, to being more risk-averse, frustrated, overwhelmed, and hesitant. And from the outside it would appear that these feelings were inevitable, as the circumstances of our business changed as we grew, but I now know that no matter what the circumstances of our business were, I was in control of how I thought about it, how I felt about it, and how I responded to the challenges. This is because our brains interpret what we see in the world via a thought. This thought then generates an emotion for us. This emotion drives our actions. And our actions create our results. And the most important part of this—we get to choose how we think about things. So, no matter what happened in our business, I could choose how I wanted to think about it.

So why is this even useful to know? Because certain emotions drive us to do or not do certain actions in our businesses, even if we know that the particular action will create the result we want. For example, we might know that we need to close a client on a particular deal to generate the monetary result we want in our business. But if we feel reluctant, hesitant, unconfident, scared, or doubtful, the chances of us actually picking up the phone to speak to that client are slim to none. And even if we do, we likely won't be generating the enthusiasm or the confidence that we'll need to come across in the pitch to close the deal.

Conversely, if we feel confident, calm, excited, or determined, we are much more likely to make that call, and the chances of it succeeding are much higher. Now, don't get me wrong—we can't control the universe and other people can do what they want. But in business, having thoughts that create feelings that make you continuously take actions toward the result you ultimately want, even when things don't work out the way you wanted them to, will get you to the level of success you want much faster than if your thoughts are creating feelings that are driving inaction or actions away from the result you want.

When I tried outsourcing for the first time and it didn't work out quite as I wanted it to, instead of choosing to think that it was a great learning experience and that I could apply it to the next time I tried it, I defaulted to thinking that maybe it wasn't going to work and that I should carry on doing it myself. That was it—it was just a simple, innocent thought that I let creep in, which completely altered how I felt and what actions I took in the business. And it is so easy to do because our brains have evolved to have a negativity bias. It served us when our main goal in life was survival, to think worst-case scenario thoughts, so that we acted more cautiously and didn't put our lives at risk. In the modern society we now live in, however, when we don't need to worry about being eaten by a tiger, all that the survival mode of the brain is doing is stifling our true potential.

This is why learning to manage our brain and the thoughts it has is the single most important gift we can give ourselves to enable us to truly fulfill our potential in our businesses and in our lives.

There are so many areas of business that your mindset impacts, but the top five that I believe are the mindset problems that will hold you back the most from reaching your true potential in your business are:

- Overwhelm and lack of time

- Fear of failure and challenges

- Money beliefs

- Procrastination

- Doubt and fear of rejection

Overwhelm and Lack of Time

Overwhelm is for sure one of the most frequently felt emotions when the tasks in your business are mounting and you feel like there aren't enough hours in the day to tackle it all. It is usually generated from one of or a variation of the following thoughts—"I can't fit it all in", "I don't have enough time", "I have so much to do", and "I'm so behind". You likely think that these are all true and that you are merely reporting the facts. But if you caught yourself when you were having one of these thoughts and took a moment to think about what exactly you were doing or not doing in that moment, you would likely find that you were either switching between tasks frantically, spinning in your head about what to do, procrastinating, ignoring your to-do list altogether, or focusing on tasks that give you quick wins to get those little hits of dopamine, rather than being productive on the more important tasks in your business. The result of all that—your to-do list gets longer, you still have so much to do, and you fall further behind.

The feeling of overwhelm does not serve you in your business. We, in the coaching community, describe it as an indulgent emotion. We typically lose the ability to prioritize, schedule, plan, and focus when we indulge in the emotion of overwhelm.

There are a few things you can do to break the cycle of overwhelm. When you notice you are feeling overwhelmed, stop what you are doing, take a deep breath, and try to find the thought you are having that is generating this emotion for you. Write it down. Then check it matches. When you think that thought, is overwhelm the emotion you feel? If yes, then you know you have found the cause of your problem. Now take ten deep breaths slowly (breathe in through your nose, and out through your mouth), counting each one in your head. Now try some different thoughts—"I have all the time I need", "It all doesn't need to be done right now", "I can figure out how to fit in the most important things", "I'm a badass", "I can manage this list, no problem". Take a moment to try each one and if none resonate, come up with one of your own. The key here is that your new thought needs to feel true/believable and it has to feel better. If you find a thought you like that is generating a more useful emotion like calm, determined, empowered, or in control, you should instantly start to feel better. Repeat this thought a few times in your head and then think about your day again. Ask yourself the question, "What are the top 3 things I need to get done today?" Write them down. Then ask yourself, "Which makes the most sense for me to start on now?" And then ask, "What's the next step I can take to move this closer to completion?" And then get to work.

Ultimately, you can prevent the frequency of the feeling of overwhelm by having a clear vision for your business and your life; a clear handle on your priorities, your goals, and your objectives; and a clear system, framework and formula in place that will help you focus on what's important, by deciding what tasks go where in your day, who deals with what, and when it gets dealt with. The combination of both thought work and systems will help you feel so much more in control and moving toward success in your business than if you let overwhelm drown you.

Fear of Failure and Challenges

This leads me on to when times get hard in your business. Or maybe when something doesn't work out the way you wanted it to.

This is where what you choose to define failure as, will make the biggest difference in your experience of it. If you see failure as something terrible, to be ashamed of, and you make it mean something about you personally, you will have a dreadful experience from start to finish. If, on the other hand, you view it as a positive thing, something to grow from, or you make it mean that you are pushing yourself to grow, that you can be proud that you are putting yourself out there and trying where many others are too scared to, and you are learning what doesn't work in the process, your experience of it will become much more bearable. It might still be uncomfortable, but it certainly won't result in you giving up on your dreams. It will just be an obstacle you have to overcome on your journey.

Fearing failure at the start will be a huge mental block from you reaching your goals, growing your business, and putting yourself out there. You likely won't set big goals if you fear you won't reach them and thus your whole experience will be so much smaller than it could be.

Change your perception of failure and you will change everything.

Like failure, how you deal with challenges in your business will all be based on how you view them. If you think of any challenges that face you as an opportunity to grow, improve your skills, develop yourself, evolve into the next-level person you want to be, and you believe that in overcoming them, you will have greater skills to handle other challenges in your business, your experience will be very different than if you decide that challenges shouldn't exist, or are painful, inconvenient, or are immovable obstacles to you achieving what you want.

One of the most powerful tools you learn from coaching when trying to overcome any challenges is to use questions as a way to get your brain to work to find solutions. An intelligent and empowering question gives your brain something useful to focus on, rather than allowing it to spin on negative thought loops, which is exactly what the human brain loves to do. For example, if you are stuck thinking, *I don't know how I could find someone who could help me with this*, ask yourself, "How can I find ten people who are great at this task and might want to work with me?". Immediately your brain will go to work trying to answer for you. Try it—use your brain, ask it empowering questions, and you will often find you have the tools to solve the challenge or problem within you already.

Money Beliefs

A lot of people won't have ever considered this, but how you think about money will have a huge impact on how you run your business, the risks you will be prepared to take, how you handle your finances, and ultimately how successful you will be.

Even if you have the best product/service that sells like hot cakes, if you have a poor money mindset, you could easily sabotage your own success.

The type of coaching I offer is not the manifestation/spiritual type as such ('money flows easily to me mantras…etc.'), so I can't advise on them either way, but if you are interested in these alternative views, then there are heaps of resources on the internet where you can learn about this.

The approach I take regarding money is that your underlying beliefs about money—how much you think is too much or too little and your past and present money story—are all important to dig out and address. This is because if you believe that you can't earn a certain amount per year, then you likely never will. Our brains focus on what we tell them to, so if you keep telling yourself that there is a ceiling on how much you can earn or how successful you can be, you will feel a certain way and act in a certain way and you will always be left with earnings that match up to no more than that amount. Similarly, if you think you are terrible at handling money and this makes you feel scared about handling it, you won't be motivated to look at it or be confident in taking actions regarding it, so you likely won't be keeping a close eye on expenses or profit or using it wisely in your business.

Procrastination

When you master the skill of not procrastinating in your business, your business success will explode. It is the biggest time waster and often we find ourselves procrastinating, doing things we don't actually care to be doing or like doing, to avoid the hard thing in our business that we ultimately want to get done.

In almost every single case it is because we listen to our primitive brain whose job is to direct us toward things that will give us immediate gratification and away from pain/challenge, rather than listening to our sophisticated pre-frontal cortex whose job it is to make good decisions for our long-term benefit. So, when we are sitting down at our computer, about to tackle that proposal that we know will likely give us more business, we find ourselves battling a compelling urge to move away from that hard task that we won't see the benefit from for days and toward something easier like emails or checking social media, where we get that little hit of dopamine from the false connection and sense of importance that comes from those avenues.

Setting up systems to reduce or eliminate distractions and to plan clear objectives and priorities to focus on are important to set you up for success. Boundaries around work times also help, provided you are disciplined enough to enforce them. Having deadlines and a coach or someone to hold you accountable and having a clear 'why' behind what you are working on are also highly recommended.

But really, this was one of the areas where I found hiring a life/mindset coach had the biggest impact, because **unless you are learning to keep promises to yourself and how to manage your primitive brain in that exact moment of temptation, you will constantly battle with procrastinating.**

Doubt and Fear of Rejection

Throughout your entire business journey, doubt, self-doubt, insecurities, and imposter syndrome will likely be things that you experience. If you are not careful, these can derail you from getting to the level you want in your business.

Imposter syndrome was definitely something that I battled with throughout my business journey, as I have mentioned previously, although I only came to realize it was this recently. This psychological phenomenon reflects a belief that you're inadequate and incompetent, despite evidence that indicates you're skilled and successful. An expert in the subject, Dr. Valerie Young, wrote a fascinating book on the subject (see recommended reading list) where she categorized it into five subgroups: The Perfectionist, The Superwoman/man, The Natural Genius, The Soloist, and The Expert. They each have their own characteristics, such as being a bit of a control freak and struggling to delegate, feeling you have to work hard to prove your worth, feeling shame when you don't master something the first time, believing achievements only count when you have worked solo on it, and constantly signing up for more courses because you will never feel like you know enough. Interestingly, I can identify with all five of the types, so no wonder I was struggling. Just becoming aware of the characteristics and beliefs associated with it, however, is a great first step to learning how to better manage it and prevent yourself to reacting to it when it does come up.

Even if you don't suffer from this phenomenon though, the more you put yourself out there, make claims about your expertise or your business products or services, and try to sell yourself, the more you will be stepping out of your comfort zone, opening yourself up to criticism, and thus starting the process of you looking inward at what others might find to disapprove of. And as soon as you do this, you will create doubt that you might not succeed on the level you desire.

So why do we criticize ourselves when we put ourselves out there in front of others? Why do we care so much about what other people think?

This is another primitive brain trait we inherited that is not proving to be very helpful in our businesses today—fear of rejection or disapproval from others. It's easy to see why this was useful back in the caveman days. Life was hard. Survival was not guaranteed. But it was possible to survive if you were in a tribe. You could hunt together more successfully, protect each other from danger, warn each other of danger, reproduce, share meals, and trade different skillsets for food, water, shelter, or warmth. It paid to fit in, have others like and accept us, and not be kicked out. Only the members of the tribe who were great at conforming and pleasing everyone in the tribe stayed in favor, and thus survived, to pass on the strong people-pleasing, opinion-caring genes that we all have to now manage in our new society.

The trouble now is that caring about what other people think is likely to hold us up in so many areas of our business—from not wanting to offer our products or services in the first place, to not wanting to be seen online, not speaking at events, and not actively selling ourselves. We even let the opinions of our friends and family influence whether or not we go after the life we want. Ultimately, you have to decide if you want this to be the case for you. One of my coaches always says, "Remember, other people aren't paying your bills."

Ironically, nowadays, standing out from the crowd is more likely to get you the client, get you noticed, get you the sale, earn you the money, and get you the authority. Shrinking into the crowd and playing small may mean you never get seen. **You need to be seen to sell.**

Another reason we care about what people think when we put our work into the world is that we think our work represents us and our value in the world. But our work isn't us and no matter how good our work is, our worthiness as a human doesn't change. No newborn baby is worth more than another newborn baby, yet as we get older, we confuse people's inherent worth with what they do in the world. Many people are also hesitant to put work into the world unless it is a guaranteed A+ standard, but you have to put your work out into the world in order to improve upon it and learn what you need to learn. Work on disconnecting your thoughts about who you are as a person from the work you do.

With regard to doubt, as an entrepreneur, you will frequently face times where you have to make a decision about which direction to take your business in, but you will likely not have any evidence to demonstrate that what you are choosing will reap positive results. Your primitive brain will be screaming at you about the danger of committing to something unknown and you will be flooded with uncertainty and confusion about which route to go down. This is because that part of your brain has evolved to protect you and it thinks it is doing what's best. It would rather you sit in indecision and so focuses on bringing up all the evidence it can find that will show that it might be a bad idea, i.e. how you have made bad decisions in the past, and how others may have tried the same thing and failed. As a result, you will feel your confidence in making the decision ebb away. But the fact is, while external proof that others have made the decision before you and it worked out will make it easier to think thoughts that will give you more confidence in making that decision, sometimes you will have to make decisions where you don't have any evidence that it has worked out for others before you. Or where their business was so different, so you can't see how it accurately represents what will happen for you.

Top tip here—thinking the thoughts "I don't know", "I don't know what to do", and "I don't know the right answer" will generate nothing but confusion, uncertainty, and self-doubt, and will stall your decision-making and your ultimate progress in your business. Even if you genuinely don't know what to do, if you tell yourself this you block yourself from coming up with intelligent ideas about what you could do. The truth is, nobody knows. Nobody knows how long we are each going to live, when mother nature will throw out a natural disaster, when there will be another pandemic, when we will all be living carbon neutral, or when we will have found a cure for cancer. Life is filled with uncertainty and change. We cannot control other people's actions, the weather, the economy, or the universe.

What we can do is decide for ourselves that no matter what the external circumstances will be, we will show up as the best version of ourselves, we will be committed to growing and testing and

trying new things in our business and our lives, and we will always do our best to make the decision we feel is best given what we know in the moment.

Once you have made that decision, you can also choose to always have your own back regarding the decision and whatever subsequent action you take. You can decide that you will be able to handle the consequences of that decision, that you have made the best decision you could in that moment. Because if you think about it, there is no such thing as a bad decision until you look back and consciously decide that it was a bad decision. You can decide that all the decisions you ever made in your life and your business were exactly the right decision to make, to teach you the things you now know and to get you to the place you are now at in your life.

Even if you decide later on to change the decision, you can still have your own back with regard to making the initial decision. If you commit to treat your decision-making process this way, it will make it so much easier to spend less time in confusion, uncertainty, and self-doubt, and more time making decisions that will move your business forward. Gather as much information as you can at the beginning, weigh up the two options, and then decide on the decision you will make. Decide that the decision you have made is the best one you could have chosen and commit to making it work for you.

Addressing Your Limiting Beliefs

There are two key ways to address the feeling of self-doubt that will help in not only making decisions, but in everything you attempt to do in your business.

The first is to work on generating self-confidence. This can be achieved by undertaking simple exercises like writing an accomplishment log of all the things you have achieved in your life to date. Include all the things, from little to big, and acknowledge the part you played in them all. Particularly note the things you struggled with, failed the first time at, or had negative comments from others on and achieved anyway. Remembering that you have failed before, been judged before, and been okay despite it, will massively help build your self-confidence toward trying new things. When you truly feel self-confident, every single part of setting up and running a business is made easier and more enjoyable—e.g. decision-making, turning an idea into reality, becoming more visible in your marketing, asking for the sale, overcoming challenges.

The second way to deal with self-doubt, when you can't seem to muster up the feeling of self-confidence, is to generate courage. As Susan Jeffers so eloquently put it, "Feel the fear, and do it anyway." Remember that the only reason you are feeling self-doubt and fear of taking action is that your primitive brain is confused. It thinks that what you are attempting to do is life-threatening and it is only trying to protect you. Work on building that courage muscle, get a coach to help you if you need to. It will be well worth the investment, I promise. In the words of Suzy Kassem, "Doubt kills more dreams than failure ever will."

Beginner's Mindset

I want to touch on your mindset at the start of your journey here. Just merely setting out on your business journey will be particularly hard for some of you, but it will be made even harder if you have the wrong mindset starting out.

The first thing to keep in mind is that it is not going to be smooth sailing. We like to refer to it, in the coaching world, as the 50:50. 50% of what you will experience running your business will be fantastic, and you will be able to feel self-pride, accomplishment, contentment, and excitement. The other 50% will be made up of frustration, disappointment, annoyance, discomfort, fear, doubt, confusion, desperation, and worry. You can't renegotiate this percentage either. Why? Because each positive emotion has an opposing negative emotion. The reason we know how good the positive emotion is, is because we have experienced the contrast. You really won't get to experience how good it can be when you achieve success in your business if you haven't tasted the contrast of how disappointing it is when something goes wrong. So, it's no problem that it is 50:50 good and bad. It's only a problem if you are arguing with this reality and expecting it to be smooth sailing all the way. Being willing to accept this reality—there will be tough times and there will be jobs that you will have to do that you won't like, but if you are willing to do it in order to have the experience of being your own business owner, it will mean that you are more likely to push through the crappy times and fully experience and enjoy the better times.

The second thing to keep in mind is your 'why'—the reason you are doing it in the first place. This will help remind you why it's worth sticking with it through the bad times.

The third thing to remember is to have a beginner's mindset. Allow yourself to put B+ work out in the world and be compassionate with yourself if it comes back to bite you. You are, after all, a beginner, and we all have to start somewhere. Never make your slip ups mean that you won't ever get to the level you want.

The fourth thing to remember is to make sure you take time to celebrate your wins along the way. We are often so impatient to get to our goals, yet as soon as we reach them, we take little to no time basking in our glory before we yearn to climb onto the next step of the ladder. This is similar to the 'grass is always greener' mentality that gets a lot of people into trouble, because they are always chasing a moving target. It's not fun to go through your life chasing this, as you will never feel satisfied. Make sure that when you achieve your goals, you take the time to enjoy what you have accomplished. Think about what struggles you conquered in order to overcome those challenges to get to that point. Think about how you have grown, what you have learned, and what you enjoyed. **It really is about enjoying the journey, so don't make the mistake of missing the best part.**

Finally, above all else, recognize when your mindset about your business situation is negative and reframe it to be more positive. There is no downside. Even if we take bigger risks, push ourselves more because we think we will get a positive outcome, and we then don't get that positive outcome, if we still view that specific outcome as a valuable learning experience along the way to figuring out what will work, then we can't go wrong.

The fact is that when we have a positive attitude, we are much more likely to feel motivated to take the actions that will give us the results we want. From a negative attitude of 'this won't work', we will likely feel discouraged, take half committed action, and then get crappy results.

So, if there is one thing I would recommend, above all else, it is to take time each day to write down your thoughts on a particular task or problem you are trying to solve and see if the thought is negative. If it is, figure out a better, more positive thought you believe that will have you creating action toward the results you want to create in your business. Don't underestimate the power of these sneaky negative thoughts and emotions in holding you back in your business.

Learning to Manage Your Brain

The main challenge I found with learning to manage my brain is that sometimes we aren't even aware of our thoughts and how they are creating the results in our lives. Some are thoughts we don't even like, but that have been fed to us through societal 'norms', our upbringings, and other people's opinions. It is also impossible sometimes to separate the thoughts from the facts of the situation when you are in the thick of it. And often, when you are living in your own mind drama, you won't be able to see that there is an alternative way to look at the problem at hand. That's where having an external coach can help so much.

It was only when I found life/mindset coaching that I was able to get a perspective on my mindset and how I was approaching certain situations, and then I truly saw why I was creating what I was creating in my life and in my business. The result, I cleaned up my thinking, overcame my limiting beliefs, removed any blocks I had, and I took actions that moved our business in the direction I wanted it to go in a calm and confident manner. I finally invested in myself, I got more organized, I decided to simplify my systems, I asked for help in areas that I struggled with. I investigated the legalities and process for hiring and then hired help to free up some of my time. I took a course in marketing and sales, and I overhauled my strategy. I invested in further improvements on-site that would generate long term rewards, and I generated the self-confidence that I could make the business suit my lifestyle and still be profitable. I wrote this book and I became an LCS Certified life and business coach to other struggling female entrepreneurs, and I haven't looked back. Are there still challenges and things we can improve upon in our businesses? Absolutely. Is everything exactly how I want it to be going forward? No. But now I see the challenges as doable and great learning experiences, rather than as inconvenient obstacles, and it has made all the difference. I genuinely believe there is no better investment for you, your family, or your business, than to invest in your mental health and get a life/mindset coach.

Action Prompts

- Check in with how often you indulge in the feeling of overwhelm. Start noticing it. Check your life design, your strategies, and then work on practicing those alternative thoughts to take you out of it

- Consider your attitude around failure and challenges. Can you reframe it?

- Dive into your own money beliefs. What is the story you tell yourself around why you earn what you earn?

- Tackle procrastination by setting up systems, eliminating distractions, planning clear objectives, setting priorities, and formulating boundaries

- Recognize the signs of imposter syndrome when they show up

- Practice building self-confidence through journaling and creating an achievement log

- Set yourself mini scary challenges to help develop your 'courage muscle'

- Work on your beginner mindset

- Remember your 'why' for starting your business in the first place

- Accept that the journey will be 50% positive, 50% negative

- Celebrate your wins

- Research how you can best learn the tools to better observe and manage your mind, either by studying them independently or hiring a coach you click with

- Commit to working through any mindset blocks that you have which are obvious already with a coach

- Build a daily habit of self-coaching and problem solving using empowering questions and gratitude journaling

CONCLUSION

I wrote this book because I wanted to share my knowledge and the lessons I learned on my journey of becoming a first-time business owner, so you don't have to make the same mistakes I did along the way. Don't get me wrong, I wouldn't change what I experienced for the world, as it has shaped who I am today. But it is usually easier and far quicker to learn from others' mistakes, than your own, if you can.

While I don't believe there is a one-size, fits-all approach to business, I do think that the key lessons I learned can be applied to any business starting out, so I really hope that you will have been able to take something from each chapter, the action prompts, and my own experiences, and will be able to apply them to your journey toward creating the business you want. I believe that you can start and run a successful business, if you commit to it. You just need to get the foundations right and your brain working with you, rather than against you. **If I can do it, so can you.**

NEXT STEPS

If you are now all in on making your business work for you, please go ahead and download my free Actionable Steps Workbook PDF from https://kirstyknightcoaching.com/first-time-entrepreneur/, where you can work through each of the action prompts within it and check them off as you go.

I also host a lovely and supportive community on Facebook for female entrepreneurs in their business journey, from right at the start to scaling to six figures. We talk business, money, marketing, productivity, and mindset. Search for the "Ladies Small Business Growth Community" on Facebook. We would love to have you join. Alternatively, get involved with me on Instagram You can find my coaching business online at www.KirstyKnightCoaching.com and you will find links to my Instagram and Facebook on my website.

Regardless of whether or not you want to join us in our Facebook group or follow me on Instagram, or you want any further support from me, I want to hear your business success stories! I hope you will send me a note when you take that leap or overhaul your business, telling me how you are doing and how your life has changed as a result of becoming an entrepreneur. And once you get going, if you are struggling with making your business or your brain work for you, and you would like me to help you, get in touch. I'd be happy to help.

Here's to you becoming an entrepreneur!

Kirsty Knight

RECOMMENDED READING LIST

Millionaire Success Habits, by Dean Graziosi

Feel the Fear and Do it Anyway, by Susan Jeffers

Profit First, by Mike Michalowicz

The Paradox of Choice, by Barry Schwartz

7 Strategies for Wealth and Happiness, by Jim Rohn

The Secret Thoughts of Successful Women, by Dr. Valerie Young

Expert Secrets, by Russell Brunson

ACKNOWLEDGEMENTS

I just want to say a huge thank you to my fabulous editor, Hannah Magnusson from Great Grey Editorial, who helped bring this project to life for me.

I am also thankful for The Self-Publishing School Team and Community as a whole for guiding me through a completely foreign process to me, and for putting me in contact with all the other important people who have helped me get this out to the rest of the world—Lise Cartwright, Debbie Lum and Danijela from Cutting Edge Studio.

Looking forward to doing the next one!

ABOUT THE AUTHOR

Kirsty Knight is an LCS certified life and business coach who is on a mission to help other ambitious, hard-working women who feel stuck in their business, uncover what is holding them back and objectively figure out what needs to change in order for them to create a business and life they love!

Far from the woo-woo, spiritual, law-of-attraction stuff out there, Kirsty combines coaching tools grounded in cognitive psychology-based techniques with her own ever-evolving business knowledge and experiences to help women come up with a practical strategy for business success, without sacrificing their enjoyment in life.

When not helping women in their businesses, or working on her own businesses, Kirsty can be found either getting stuck in a random DIY project, attempting to surf at one of her favorite Welsh beaches, or messing about on the river in her rowing boat with her long-term partner Andrew and their giant Newfoundland cross puppy Diesel.

Can You Help?

Thank You For Reading My Book!

I really appreciate all of your feedback, and I love hearing what you have to say.

I need your input to make the next version of this book and my future books better.

Please leave me an honest review on Amazon letting me know what you thought of the book.

Thanks so much!

Kirsty Knight

Printed in Great Britain
by Amazon